Praise for *Equal Is Equal, Fair Is Fair*

"The author's well-researched historical examination of our State Constitution's common benefits clause is a delightful reminder that, even though issues change, Vermont's way of dealing with them has never faltered. Long championed since the days of our founding by progressive thinkers of all political stripes, this clause must always be the fulcrum upon which competing civil rights interests are balanced. Gilbert's fascinating behind-the-scenes look at three of the most contentious issues of our time gives the reader insight into how future debates will likely be framed. Everyone interested in Vermont history should have this book on their bookshelf, especially those politicians and lawyers who may end up at the forefront of the next contentious discussion."

> – Joe Benning, state senator and minority leader, attorney, former chair Vermont Human Rights Commission

"Our nation's founders didn't give us many answers about equity, but they gave us ways to keep asking questions. And Vermonters keep asking. On three pressing issues, Allen Gilbert traces Vermont's unique, centuries-old Q&A among the executive, legislative, and judicial branches of government, and offers us a front-row seat in the ongoing and urgent conversations that comprise our state, local, and very personal decision-making."

> – Susan Clark, co-author of two books on deliberative democracy (*Slow Democracy* and *All Those in Favor*), community development advocate, and town meeting moderator

"In crisp prose supported by extensive, meticulous research, Allen Gilbert has traced the legal and social history of a basic Vermont ideal — that everyone, on a fair and equal basis, is entitled to the benefits of society. Vermont has succeeded in realizing that equality in two areas: paying for children's education and recognizing the marriage rights of homosexuals. But Gilbert asks why this has not been accomplished in a third area, health care, despite numerous efforts to do so. From the common benefits clause of the Vermont Constitution to the most recent legislation, this book is a brisk and highly readable analysis of an idea that is central to the Vermont experience — and the Vermont soul."

> – Tom Slayton, former newspaper journalist,
> Vermont Press Bureau chief, and *Vermont Life* editor

"Allen Gilbert's short, but highly provocative, examination of the application of the Vermont Constitution's common benefits clause is extremely well-researched and makes for engaging reading. Gilbert brings to life the tensions brought by the two game-changing Vermont Supreme Court decisions on school funding and same-sex marriage. His explanation of the historical roots of common benefits as set out by then-Chief Justice Amestoy in the *Baker* decision, then his analysis of the application of that right to same-sex marriage through two other justices' opinions in the case, is quite compelling. Comparing the leading cases of *Brigham* and *Baker* with Vermont's failure to achieve health care for all prompts the thought of pursuing a constitutional amendment to truly make health care a human right to be enjoyed by all Vermonters."

> – Robert Appel, former chief of the Civil Rights Unit
> of the Vermont Attorney General's Office, state
> defender general, and executive director of the
> Vermont Human Rights Commission

"Allen Gilbert has had a front row seat to history in Vermont and the U.S. *Equal is Equal, Fair is Fair* chronicles how Vermonters led the nation in establishing groundbreaking laws for marriage equality, equitable education, and universal health care. Gilbert is no bystander to this history. As longtime head of the Vermont ACLU, Gilbert writes with intimacy and empathy about the characters and issues at the center of these struggles. This is an engaging inside story of how movements for social justice that began in a small state have led to big social change."

> – David Goodman, author and host,
> *The Vermont Conversation*

"Allen Gilbert has written a book of great importance, timeliness, and originality. Current and future discussions of equity in Vermont are bound to reference the ideas he so eloquently advances. Vermont is perceived by many to be in the vanguard of progressive ideals and actions, reflective of its commitment to equity and inclusion. The state's foundational value of equity, Gilbert teaches us, is rooted in its unique constitution. But movement toward greater equality in Vermont is not easy, nor is it a given. Gilbert explores Vermont's recent tumultuous history of the road to educational finance reform and marriage equality, illuminating the struggle to implement Vermonters' desire, sometimes latent, to promote the common good. His compelling reflection reminds us that the journey toward equity endures, as the state grapples with the still elusive goal of health care equality, the unequal effects of climate change and COVID-19, racial and gender inequality, and childhood deprivation. Though the work is not done, Gilbert's narrative illustrates how Vermont's history and culture bid us to continue to advocate for and implement policies that promote the common good."

> – Stephanie Seguino, University of Vermont economics
> professor, co-author of "Driving While Black and Brown
> in Vermont" report, and former president of the
> International Association for Feminist Economics

Praise for *Equal Is Equal, Fair Is Fair* (cont.)

"Allen Gilbert brings alive critical chapters in Vermont's recent history, weaving together the fights for equal education opportunity and marriage equality. Even those of us who lived through these historic triumphs will learn new details and gain greater perspective. A key takeaway is that there is no guarantee that fairness, equity, and equality will win out. It takes everyday heroes to stand up and speak out and challenge the status quo. Gilbert tells those personal stories and he, too, is one of those everyday heroes. Gilbert's reminder of the power of the Vermont Constitution to provide greater protections than the U.S. Constitution is especially timely as the U.S. Supreme Court tacks to the right. It is truly fascinating to read how a clause written into the Pennsylvania Constitution in 1776 led to marriage equality in Vermont more than two centuries later. Gilbert knows his stuff and tells it well."

– Chris Graff, radio, TV, and print journalist,
Vermont AP bureau chief for 27 years and Vermont
Public Television's *Vermont This Week* host for 15 years;
vice president for communications at National Life Group

EQUAL IS EQUAL, FAIR IS FAIR

EQUAL IS EQUAL, FAIR IS FAIR

*Vermont's Quest for Equity
in Education Funding,
Marriage Rights,
and Health Care*

By Allen Gilbert

With a Foreword by David Moats

ONION
RIVER
PRESS

Burlington, Vermont

For permissions and more information regarding *Equal Is Equal, Fair Is Fair* contact the author at **hallengilbert@gmail.com** or visit **equalisequal.com**

Front cover (detail) and back cover art: Unidentified maker, *Justice,* ca. 1800. Pine, wood, and metal, 120 in. Collection of Shelburne Museum, museum purchase, 1950, 1961-1.299. Photography by Andy Duback.

Interior art (details): Unidentified maker, *Justice,* ca. 1800. Pine, wood, and metal, 120 in. Collection of Shelburne Museum, museum purchase, 1950, 1961-1.299. Photography by Allen Gilbert.

Photo of the author: Elizabeth Hewitt/VT Digger

Book design: Laughing Bear Associates, Montpelier, Vermont

Onion River Press
191 Bank Street, Burlington, VT 05401

ISBN: 978-1-949066-51-7
Library of Congress Control Number: 2020910456
Publisher's Cataloging-in-Publication Data:
Names: Gilbert, Allen, 1951-, author.
Title: Equal is equal , fair is fair : Vermont's quest for equity in education funding , same-sex marriage, and health care / by Allen Gilbert; foreword by David Moats.
Description: Includes bibliographical references. | Burlington, VT: Onion River Press, 2020.
Identifiers: LCCN: 2020910456 | ISBN: 978-1-949066-51-7
Subjects: LCSH Vermont--Politics and government. | Education--Vermont--Finance. | Same-sex marriage--Vermont. | Same-sex marriage--Law and legislation--Vermont. | Medical care, Cost of--Vermont. | Health planning--Vermont. | Law reform--Vermont--Citizen participation. | Political participation--Vermont. | BISAC HISTORY / United States / State & Local / New England | LAW / Government / State, Provincial & Municipal | POLITICAL SCIENCE / Civil Rights | POLITICAL SCIENCE / Political Process / Political Advocacy
Classification: LCC JK3095 .G55 2020 | DDC 320.9743--dc23

For Robert Gensburg

*I have known no person in my life
who better understood and fought
harder for equity and fairness.*

Contents

Foreword

By David Moats

Vermont experienced a sort of constitutional revolution in the 1990s, but it was a revolution with roots reaching back to the founding of the state. Allen Gilbert was present for all of it, and he has written a searching examination of the history and meaning of events in Vermont with profound implications for the nation.

Gilbert's treatise, *Equal Is Equal, Fair Is Fair,* explores in detail events that dominated the news in the late 1990s and early 2000s. First came a decision by the Vermont Supreme Court in the famous *Brigham* decision requiring the state legislature to create a new educational funding system adhering to principles of equity for all Vermonters. Second came the even more famous *Baker* decision requiring the legislature to find a way to extend the rights and benefits of marriage to same-sex couples. From the distance of 20 years, it's worth reminding ourselves of the profound way these decisions shook the state, requiring citizens and policymakers alike to wrestle with fundamentally important moral and political questions.

Gilbert then asks a provocative question: If principles of equity demanded action on the issues of education and marriage, why have the same principles not succeeded in creating comprehensive reforms establishing equity in health care for all Vermonters?

Gilbert's work provides a thorough recounting of these events and the arguments that propelled them. But at a deeper level he traces the origins and meaning of the issues all the way back to the beginning of the state's history, exploring the origins of the Vermont Constitution, which was modeled on the Pennsylvania Constitution and remains one of the most radical state constitutions in safeguarding citizens' rights. He examines the shared history that surrounds us in what he calls a "cultural cocoon," which consists of "long chains of beliefs, actions, and interrelationships" reaching back to the revolutionary values prevailing at the founding of the nation.

So it was that the common benefits clause of the Vermont Constitution became "a key from the eighteenth country" that was used "to turn on a neglected engine of equity" in the twentieth century. The common benefits clause says "that government is, or ought to be, instituted for the common benefit, protection, and security of the people, nation, or community, and not for the particular emolument or advantage of any single person, family, or set of persons, who are a part only of that community . . . ." As Gilbert shows, this clause was the key in helping Vermonters discover constitutional rights that had been there all the time.

The history lessons contained in Gilbert's work are surprising and informative. The state's struggle to achieve fairness in education funding has a history going back to the 19th century. In fact, a statewide property tax for education existed between 1890 and 1931. Thus, he shows that the struggle for equity is not a historical aberration but part of a continuing effort going back more than 200 years to vindicate the values underpinning the state's democracy.

The struggle to provide health care for all Vermonters also has a long history, and it continues to this day. Gilbert shows how that effort has proven more difficult because there is nothing in the state's constitution establishing that access to health care must be considered a right requiring equitable treatment for all. Thus, state policymakers have had to wrestle with what he calls "the tension between knowing what is right and doing what is right."

Gilbert underscores several important ideas as he examines these questions. He describes how states, including Vermont, began to turn to state constitutions when it appeared the U.S. Supreme Court could no longer be relied on to protect equal rights. Thus, it was the Vermont Constitution, rather than the Fourteenth Amendment of the U.S. Constitution, that was instrumental in both the education and marriage cases.

Gilbert also highlights the judicial approach of Jeffrey Amestoy, the former chief justice of the Vermont Supreme Court who wrote the unanimous decision in the *Baker* case. Amestoy has delineated a form of constitutional pragmatism that takes into account the role of the judiciary within the larger political context. Amestoy has said that when courts make decisions, they are like a family modifying a house while continuing to live in it. Courts are not architects from outside the system. They dwell within the system, and practical steps to improve the house while maintaining its integrity are the mark of constitutional pragmatism. Amestoy's view was not shared by everyone on the Vermont Supreme Court; two justices wrote concurring opinions differing with Amestoy on these questions. But Amestoy's form of pragmatism has yielded a thoughtful and useful form of judicial restraint.

Gilbert's work is perhaps most useful in capturing the historical continuity of the long struggle for equity in Vermont. As a journalist and author, I, too, was in the middle of these events, and reading his summation reminded me of the drama, the complexity, and importance of the issues at stake. It's a good lesson in Vermont history, and it shows how the history happening today is only the latest chapter of an enduring and essential struggle.

Introduction

This is a book about fairness and equity, issues Vermonters have grappled with throughout the state's history. I focus specifically on three topics, rooted in these issues, that have dominated Vermont's politics during the last twenty-five years: school funding, same-sex marriage, and health care. Vermont has made landmark advances in two of the three while gaining impressive, though less than satisfying, results in the third.

I started my research for this book shortly after retiring as executive director of the American Civil Liberties Union of Vermont in 2016. I had begun the job in 2004. Twelve years later, I felt a need to untangle a lifetime of questions about the concept of equity — the notion that we're all created equal — and about government's role in ensuring we're treated fairly.

An interest in notions of accountability, justice, and fairness has animated my work over forty years as a journalist, a teacher, and a civil liberties advocate. I've been lucky to have lived and worked in Vermont for most of those years; the state has been a cauldron of equity activities. The *Brigham* decision in 1997 led to school funding equity. The *Baker* decision in 1999 led to same-sex marriage rights. Through these times, Vermont struggled with creating a health care system that provides all citizens with adequate medical care, an issue that continues to challenge us.

In doing my research I recognized another important connection between my past and present interests. I was raised in rural Pennsylvania, in the Pennsylvania Dutch section of the state. It's hard to grow up there and not wonder who exactly the "Penn" in Pennsylvania was. On trips to Philadelphia, my brothers and I would crane our necks to see his statue, which topped City Hall. (Until 1985, public sentiment dictated that no building in the city could rise higher than his hat.[1]) It was in fourth grade, when every Pennsylvania school child was given a textbook called *Living Together in Pennsylvania,* that I learned why this man stood so tall atop Philadelphia's City Hall, his right arm outstretched and pointing as if to direct those beneath him.

William Penn was a Quaker from a wealthy British family. He founded Pennsylvania as a haven of tolerance and equality at a time when the existing British colonies in North America were decidedly intolerant, especially concerning religion. A dreamer as a young man (and jailed for a time in the Tower of London for his Quaker beliefs), Penn became an enlightened proprietor of the vast acreage given his family as payment of a royal debt. He insisted that generous treaties be made with Native Americans who lived in the territory. He sent agents through war-torn areas of Europe to recruit settlers looking to escape the death and destruction of religious wars between Catholics and Protestants in the 1600s.

Penn died in 1718. The idealistic vision he had established for the colony dimmed. His heirs were not the enlightened benefactors he had been, and associates he had trusted proved anything but trustworthy. Deep political rifts developed, especially between the established professional and political elite concentrated in the Philadelphia area and poor immigrants who flooded to the state and fanned out north and west from the entry port of Philadelphia. The latter were among the "upland Pennsylvanians" historians write about when describing internal political tensions at the time of the American Revolution.

I had never known the importance of the notion of "common benefits," described in the first Pennsylvania Constitution of 1776, until, in 1997, I read the briefs and opinion in the *Brigham* case, and then two years later, those in the *Baker* case. There is a direct constitutional connection between the state where I was born and the one where I've spent most of my life. It runs through the pivotal common benefits clause in the Vermont Constitution on which both the *Brigham* and *Baker* decisions are based. The clause comes directly, nearly word-for-word, from Pennsylvania's first constitution.

In this country, and particularly in Vermont, we are constantly challenged to think not just of our own good but of the common good as well. Sometimes we shine at this task; other times we create a muddled mess. There is no guarantee that fairness, equity, and equality will win out. Even when they do, there is no guarantee that the victories will be permanent.

But surrounding us like a cultural cocoon is our shared history. The Vermont Supreme Court's opinion in the *Baker* case describes long chains of beliefs, actions, and interrelationships that have placed us where we are and provided us the knowledge and skills with which we take on life's responsibilities — including civic responsibilities — and, as a state, pursue the interests we hope will bring us happiness. Within Vermont's constitutional framework lies a firm commitment to community and fairness.

To be clear, the U.S. Constitution provides a floor of rights that we all enjoy, no matter which state we live in. People in both Vermont and New Hampshire, for example, as well as in all other states, enjoy the free speech protections of the First Amendment.

An individual state, though, through its own constitution, can provide *greater* protections of rights enumerated in the U.S. Constitution — or a state can even specify other rights not mentioned there. (An example of state-enumeration of a right is privacy, which is not explicitly mentioned in the U.S. Constitution but appears in a number of state constitutions).

The result is substantial variations in how states define the rights of individuals and the authority of their states' governments.

Vermont stands out as providing heightened protection of individual rights. Several provisions of our constitution advance fair treatment of all citizens and demand that government act to ensure all citizens be treated justly. The most important of these provisions is the seventh article of the Vermont Constitution's Declaration of Rights, the common benefits clause — the clause copied from the Pennsylvania constitution. The clause states that "government is, or ought to be, instituted for the common benefit, and security of the people, nation, or community, and not for the particular emolument or advantage of any single man, family, or set of men, who are a part only of that community. . . ." (The text of the full articles in the Pennsylvania and Vermont constitutions with the common benefits clause can be found at the end of this introduction.)

Everyone must be treated equally, in other words, when government provides a benefit to its citizens.

Vermont's copying of the Pennsylvania language was no coy theft or unintended plagiarism. The state's founders specifically wanted their constitution to be nearly identical to that of Pennsylvania.

The founders' decision was a tactical one, based on the advice of a friend and mentor of Ethan Allen, Dr. Thomas Young of Philadelphia. Young was recognized as an astute observer of the politics of the young nation. When a delegation from Vermont failed in 1777 to persuade the Continental Congress to recognize Vermont's petition for statehood, Young agreed to meet with the delegates to strategize about how to make a better case the next time they appeared before Congress.

Young said that Vermonters needed to show that they were ready and able to form a working government and to be accepted as the new country's fourteenth state. The first step, he said, was to develop a constitution. He suggested the recently passed Pennsylvania Constitution as a model. It was widely recognized as the most progressive of all the states' constitutions.

The Vermonters followed his advice. They copied entire sections of the Pennsylvania Constitution to affirm the values they were told the most respected thinkers of the time held — and which they shared.[2]

Other states did the same. But their constitutions were later amended (as was Pennsylvania's), the boldness of the Revolutionary War-era language diluted or, even in some cases, eliminated. Not so with the Vermont Constitution. It is the least amended of any state constitution in the country. Vermont is still governed by progressive language on individual rights written in the immediate afterglow of the colonies' break with Great Britain.

The draft of the Vermont Constitution was first reviewed and accepted by a convention in Windsor in 1777. It was revised in 1786. A few more, minor changes were made in 1793 when Vermont agreed to drop language about claims against New York based on prior land grant disputes; deletion of this language in the constitution was a condition of Vermont's acceptance as the country's fourteenth state.

The power behind the straightforward assertion, in Article 7 of the Vermont Constitution, that benefits provided by the state have to be made available to citizens on an equal basis, wasn't apparent for some time. And on the federal level, even though passage by Congress of the Fourteenth Amendment in 1868 promised equal treatment to all citizens, continued discrimination against African-Americans made this promise hollow. It wasn't until the mid-twentieth century that the U.S. Supreme Court, under Chief Justice Earl Warren, began applying Fourteenth-Amendment "equal protection" arguments in a number of areas involving individual rights (such as schooling, voting, reproductive choices, and equal access to facilities serving the public).

This changed in the latter years of the twentieth century, however, as appointments of more conservative federal judges and justices resulted in a retreat by the U.S. Supreme Court from expansive rulings on equity. Vermont judges were encouraged to look to the state's constitution for broader protections of basic rights. This encouragement came from the Vermont Supreme Court itself.

In a 1985 decision, Vermont Supreme Court Justice Thomas Hayes ordered lawyers defending a man stopped and arrested by police to go back and do more work on the legal briefs they had presented to the court. The lawyers had raised the possibility that the Vermont Constitution offered stronger protections of a defendant's rights than the U.S. Constitution, yet the lawyers hadn't fully developed their argument. This was a disservice to the defendant, Hayes said; Vermont lawyers needed to consider the range of rights available to defendants.

"This generation of Vermont lawyers has an unparalleled opportunity to aid in the formulation of a state constitutional jurisprudence that will protect the rights and liberties of our people, however the philosophy of the United States Supreme Court may ebb and flow," Hayes wrote for the court. Occurring at "this time of the post-Warren counter-revolution," he said, was a "resurrection of federalism and state judicial independence."[3]

Hayes's opinion attracted national attention. Like the ancient VW Beetle that Woody Allen cranked to life in the 1973 movie *Sleeper,* Vermont's constitution was called on to provide the necessary judicial energy for protection of individual rights. The language in the hand-written eighteenth-century document became a time-capsule gift to modern Vermonters.

Justice Hayes didn't live long enough (he died in 1987) to see how that stored energy would be tapped to bring about important changes in Vermont.

The *Brigham v. State* case on school funding was brought by the American Civil Liberties Union of Vermont. The litigation grew out of frustration that the legislature was unable to fix the state's deficient school funding mechanism. The "Foundation Formula" then in place was not providing all schools with the financial support they needed. The basic problems were overreliance on local property taxes and the state's reluctance to make more equitable the access to the funds that towns needed to operate their schools.

The *Baker v. State* case on marriage rights was brought by lawyers representing three same-sex couples who had been denied marriage licenses. The gay rights movement was exploding around the country, and numerous national and state groups looked to the courts as an avenue to equity. Vermont's *Baker* decision was the first judicial assertion by any U.S. court that the benefits of marriage had to be made available to all couples regardless of their sexual orientation.

The effort for health care equity has taken a different course. The state has never established a medical services program for all Vermonters. Asserting a common benefits constitutional right of equal access is difficult when a universal-access benefit hasn't yet been created. So, health care reform advocates have instead pressed for political action through the state legislature. The absence of a judicial mandate to spur swift progress toward their goal is a significant hindrance.

Nonetheless, the quest for health care equity is based on the same sentiment underlying the court decisions on school funding and marriage. Equal is equal, and fair is fair.

•

A note on terms

I use the word "equity" throughout this book to mean "equality of access" to a benefit or privilege provided by government. I do so because the word "equity" describes a principle and process while "equality" describes a result.

The distinction may seem insignificant at first, and indeed the words are often used interchangeably. But as I was writing this book, I saw that we sometimes seek an "equality" that is elusive and confusing. This came up consistently during my exploration of children's school opportunities. The phrase "education equality" is used in various ways to mean different things. For some, "education equality" means that the same academic courses and extracurricular activities are offered in all schools. For others, it means that all schools provide a broad range of academic and nonacademic offerings that allow all children to flourish in their own ways. And for still others, it means that minimum student test scores are mandated so that all children achieve at some uniformly high level. In the *Brigham* case, however, "education equality" is seen through the lens of money, and means equal access to school funds for all Vermont school districts.

"Equity" means equal treatment of everyone. A principle is identified and a process put in place to achieve it. No result is guaranteed because of that equity. But if a government provides tools or resources — for example, to help students succeed in school, for couples to have an established long-term relationship, or patients to recover from an illness — everyone must have equal access to those tools and resources. What happens next when those tools and resources are applied is not guaranteed. We are unique individuals with a range of differences. Tools and resources are designed to increase our chances of success, but they don't ensure that success will occur for everyone on the same basis. Even with equity to resources provided by government, some students will achieve higher test scores than others, some couples will have more successful marriages than others, and some patients will live longer lives than others. The results of equity, in other words, are not necessarily equal.

•

The articles in the Pennsylvania and Vermont constitutions containing the common benefits clause

The full text of Article V in the 1776 Pennsylvania Constitution's Declaration of Rights states:

> *That government is, or ought to be, instituted for the common benefit, protection and security of the people, nation or community; and not for the particular emolument or advantage of any single man, family, or set of men, who are a part only of that community; And that the community hath an indubitable, unalienable and indefeasible right to reform, alter, or abolish*

government in such manner as shall be by that community judged most conducive to the public weal.

The full text of Article VI in the 1777 Vermont Constitution's Declaration of Rights states:

That government is, or ought to be, instituted for the common benefit, protection, and security of the people, nation or community; and not for the particular emolument or advantage of any single man, family or set of men, who are a part only of that community; and that the community hath an indubitable, unalienable and indefeasible right to reform, alter, or abolish, government, in such manner as shall be, by that community, judged most conducive to the public weal.

No changes — except substituting the gender-neutral terms "single person, family, or set of persons" for the original gender-specific "single man, family or set of men," in the 1990s — have ever been made to the "common benefits" portion of the article in Vermont's Constitution. Changes *were* made to the second part of the article, regarding changing government, when revisions were made to the Vermont Constitution in 1786. Vermont narrowed the right of changing government to *reforming* or *altering* it; the right to *abolish* government was dropped. Also, the number of the article containing Vermont's common benefits clause changed. It started out as Article VI in 1777, but it became Article VII in 1786 when a new article guaranteeing a right to "remedy at law" was added as Article IV and the subsequent articles were renumbered.

To give full credit to all contributors to the common benefits language, it should be noted that Pennsylvania, when drafting its constitution, drew on Sections 3 and 4 of the Virginia Declaration of

Rights, which had been adopted by the Virginia House of Burgesses a few months before the Pennsylvania Constitution was finalized in 1776.

- The text of the 1776 Pennsylvania Constitution is online at https://avalon.law.yale.edu/18th_century/pa08.asp#1 Accessed April 15, 2020.

- The text of the Virginia Declaration of Rights is online at http://edu.lva.virginia.gov/online_classroom/shaping_the_constitution/doc/declaration_rights Accessed March 29, 2020.

- The text of the Vermont Constitution (the original 1777 version, and the revised versions of 1786 and 1793) can be found online at https://sos.vermont.gov/vsara/learn/constitution/1777-constitution/ Accessed March 29, 2020.

- The current Vermont Constitution, which includes all gender-neutrality changes, is online at https://legislature.vermont.gov/statutes/constitution-of-the-state-of-vermont/ Accessed March 29, 2020.

Chapter 1

School Funding Restructuring

*B*ehind every legal case is a person and a story. The school funding
case filed in 1995 in Vermont Superior Court in Hyde Park was
Brigham v. State of Vermont. *Although there were thirteen plaintiffs,
the "lead" plaintiff was Amanda Brigham — her surname came first,
alphabetically, in the list of plaintiffs, and so the file created by the court
was "Brigham." I always felt it was fitting that a lawsuit that broke new
legal ground in an important education issue took the name of an eight-
year-old. Once the Vermont Supreme Court decision in the case was
handed down two years later, legislators explaining a school funding
issue began to say that "Brigham requires this" or "Brigham doesn't
allow that." I smiled to think how appropriate it was that a child from a
rural Addison County farm town seemed to be telling adults what to do
when it came to education.*

*Amanda was the daughter of Carol and Rusty Brigham of Whiting,
a hard-working couple who struggled to keep the family farm going,
but ended up having to work off the farm as well, to make ends meet.
Carol served on the Whiting School Board. She knew how hard it was to
balance the school's budget. The town was property-poor, and residents'*

incomes were below the state average. There was nothing fancy about the small school in the village that served kids in kindergarten through sixth grade.

Amanda was squirming in a decidedly adult-size chair when I met her in the summer of 1995 at the Lamoille County Courthouse. Her mother introduced us, explaining that my school was also involved in the lawsuit — we were a plaintiff, like her. Amanda said, "Hello," after prompting from her mom; Carol whispered to me that she was shy. I tried to put myself in her shoes, pondering what it would be like if my mother and I had one day gotten into our car and driven eighty-five miles from the small town where I was growing up to attend something called a "hearing" to change things so schools worked better for all kids. It's hard to know how much any eight-year-old can understand of a complicated legal case.

There was something about the way Amanda squirmed that late summer day, though, her feet unable to touch the courthouse's wooden floor but her eyes roaming the school-like room, with the judge's bench, the lawyers' tables, and rows of seats, that told me she may not now understand what was happening, but that at some point in the future she would. She'd know she was part of history that day.

As Amanda grew older, so did her confidence. After elementary school in Whiting, she went to the regional high school in Brandon and then out of state for college. Carol and I would often meet at state education functions, and she would update me on what Amanda was doing. I felt immensely proud when Amanda gained bachelor's and master's degrees in sports management, worked at universities in Pennsylvania and New York, and then returned to Vermont for a job at Norwich University. She and her husband bought their first house, in Northfield, and by 2017 she had become an aunt. When I retired from the ACLU in 2016, Amanda and her mom drove from Whiting to Montpelier for my going-away party. "I get it now," her smile said to me when we reminisced about the lawsuit and her role in it.

Looking back to our first meeting at the Lamoille County Courthouse, it seems like Amanda's involvement in the lawsuit was destiny, for the Brigham family's dedication to equity is generational. Her mother served on school boards for twenty-four years and has remained one of the fiercest defenders of student equity in Vermont. Carol Brigham's dad was a school board member for nine years and a lister for eighteen. His biggest concern as a lister was tax equity.

It's not easy being a plaintiff in a lawsuit. Amanda has never worn on her sleeve the notoriety awarded by the alphabet. Her shyness long ago gave way to a proud modesty of a young woman whose school needed help.

•

Publicly funded education for all

When "common" schools were established in America two hundred years ago, the young nation made a commitment unmatched anywhere else in the world. Americans said that every citizen in our society mattered, and that every citizen deserved an equal chance to succeed. Public schools were created to carry through on that commitment.

It's hard to appreciate how radical a step this was at the time. Beyond the broad democratic notion that everyone matters (though to be accurate, slaves and women were, admittedly, valued differently), public schools represented a vast expansion of government's role in people's lives and a huge new expenditure of public funds. It's a miracle that we ever succeeded in this endeavor. Indeed, in some states, public school advocates almost didn't succeed.

My college thesis research project was about Rhode Island's efforts to establish public schools. I became interested in the topic when I learned that schools were started in Rhode Island only after a rebellion in 1842 against the state government — an armed rebellion that resulted, for a time, in the establishment of a rival government. The "Dorr Rebellion," as it was called because of its leader, Thomas Dorr, was the result of the refusal by Rhode Island's dominant conservative faction to expand voting rights beyond property-owning white males. I was amazed to learn that any state had ever faced insurrection, and that schools figured into the resulting drama.

The Dorr government collapsed when Rhode Island citizens were horrified by the sight of cannons on the lawn of their state house and the federal government threatened to intervene if the "lawful" government was not reinstated.[4]

But even after the old political leaders returned to power, fear remained.

A new working class, made up of nonfarm laborers employed in factories, was developing in the state as industrialization took hold along the state's rivers, where water power was plentiful. Many factory workers were immigrants, new to America; most owned no property, and a large number spoke little English or were illiterate. Thoughtful conservatives recognized that these new citizens and their children couldn't be marginalized and left out of public life. Worried, though, that these citizens weren't quite ready for full participation in democracy, the state's conservative Whig Party committed to establishing a comprehensive public school system — something they had opposed before the Dorr Rebellion.

A young, energetic reformer from Connecticut, Henry Barnard, was appointed Rhode Island's first education commissioner. And so, in Rhode Island as well as in most of the rest of the country, the great public endeavor of universal free education began. (Southern states did not share the same enthusiasm for public education; in fact, legal prohibitions against educating slaves were common and schools for slaves nonexistent.)[5]

The other New England states had been early advocates of public education. Every summer, when I'm visiting in-laws in western Massachusetts, I cycle a route that takes me up from the Connecticut River Valley into the Berkshires. High on a hill, on a dirt road that rises past a dam providing water for the city of Northampton, Massachusetts, is a small building that bears a sign proudly identifying it as the "Nash Hill Schoolhouse," built in 1786.

It couldn't have been easy to live on Nash Hill in the late eighteenth century. The soils are thin and resources scarce. Yet townspeople wanted their children to read, learn their numbers, and have the skills necessary to participate in a new republic that had just negotiated its independence from Great Britain. They wanted a school, and they built one and maintained it for the next 131 years. The simple but sturdy structure served six generations of the town's children.

There are other schools in Massachusetts with a longer history. Boston Latin School was the first, established in 1635, a year before Harvard's founding.[6] Yet the tiny one-room schoolhouse on Nash Hill in a remote part of the state, a hundred miles from Boston (and only thirty miles from Vermont, which wasn't yet a part of the United States in 1786) is eloquent testimony to the value settlers placed on public education for their children.

Vermont shared the American commitment to public schools. In fact, the state's constitution proclaimed Vermonters' desire to be a leader in the effort. The Vermont Constitution of 1777 was the first of any state's constitution to promise all children access to a public education — starting with local schools in each town, continuing to a grammar school (essentially, a high school) in each of the counties, and culminating in a state university.

Chapter 2, Section 40 of the 1777 Vermont Constitution stated:

A school or schools shall be established in each town, by the legislature, for the convenient instruction of youth, with such salaries to the masters, paid by each town, making proper use of school lands in each town, thereby to enable them to instruct youth at low prices. One grammar school in each county, and one university in this State, ought to be established by direction of the General Assembly.

This language was amended in 1786. Among the changes, Section 40 was combined with Section 41 (a general section on the promotion of civic values), and advanced education options were dropped (the University of Vermont was about to be founded in Burlington).[7] This language remained the same when other revisions were made in 1793 — and largely remained the same for more than 150 years. In 1954, an amendment allowed two towns to jointly operate one school (this change was needed to avoid a constitutional challenge when a town no longer operated its own school). In 1964, an amendment broadened acceptable school ownership and operation by dropping specific mention of joint operation and substituting "other provisions" that the general assembly may permit (this change was sought by "receiving" school districts that accepted students from "sending" districts; the receiving districts wanted to retain sole governance of their school rather than have to share governance through forming a joint district). The language, after these amendments, is the current Section 68, the so-called "education clause," of Chapter 2; it retains its original 1786 title, "Laws To Encourage Virtue And Prevent Vice; Schools; Religious Activities":

> *Laws for the encouragement of virtue and prevention of vice and immorality ought to be constantly kept in force, and duly executed; and a competent number of schools ought to be maintained in each town unless the general assembly permits other provisions for the convenient instruction of youth. All religious societies, or bodies of people that may be united or incorporated for the advancement of religion and learning, or for other pious and charitable purposes, shall be encouraged and protected in the enjoyment of the privileges, immunities, and estates, which they in justice ought to enjoy, under such regulations as the general assembly of this state shall direct.*

The importance of providing all children in all towns with a free, public education became an obligation Vermont accepted as "vital." In 1860 the Vermont Supreme Court said, in the case *Williams v. School District,* that "from the earliest period in this State, the proper education of all of the children of its inhabitants has been regarded as a matter of vital interest to the State, a duty which devolved upon its government, and which should be fulfilled at the public expense."[8]

The constitutional requirement that each town provide schooling to its children established access to education as a fundamental right. (The word "ought," as used in Section 68, has been interpreted by the courts to have meant the same as "shall" in eighteenth-century

English.) The lawyers who brought the *Brigham* case in 1995 argued that this right, coupled with the common benefits guarantee in Article 7 of Chapter 1 of the state constitution, required the state to provide all of the state's children equal access to education opportunities.

This argument was like picking up a key from the eighteenth century to turn on a neglected engine of equity for today's schoolchildren.

Achievements lag aspirations

To be sure, numerous nods to school equity had been made during the years between the *Williams* decision of 1860 and the *Brigham* decision of 1997. In addresses to the legislature, a range of governors (nearly all Republicans — no Democrats were elected governor between 1855 and 1962[9]) spoke to the issue of school opportunities for the state's children.[10]

The call of Governor William Dillingham, in 1890, perhaps went the furthest — and sounds the most modern. He asked the legislature to pass a statewide property tax, the proceeds to be distributed by the state to equalize school resources across towns. "Facts" that the state's school superintendent had "brought to light in relation to the inequalities in taxation for school purposes are positively startling," Dillingham told legislators in his 1890 inaugural address. Tax rates differed among towns from seventeen cents "on the dollar of the grand list" to nearly eight times that — $1.30. Even worse disparities existed within the districts of some towns (most towns had an average of six school districts within their boundaries); the worst intra-town tax disparities were in the town of Bakersfield, where residents in one district paid seven cents on the dollar of the grand list while those in another paid \$2.15 — nearly thirty-one times more. (The "town tax rate" reported to the state was the average of a town's individual districts' rates.)

The legislature, which was presumably as startled as Dillingham by the analysis, enacted a statewide property tax of five cents on the dollar.[11] This money was then redistributed to towns based on each town's local tax base and the number of schools operating within it.

The tax, adopted in 1890, remained in effect until 1931, when it was repealed. Reasons for the repeal were threefold: 1) a complaint that property taxpayers were overburdened; 2) stress to the state's tax-raising capacity due to bonds issued for repairs to roads, bridges, and other infrastructure following the state's devastating 1927 flood; and 3) the Great Depression. Governor Stanley Wilson, in his 1933 inaugural address, expressed pride that the statewide property tax had ended. "We have succeeded in relieving our grand list from all direct state taxes," he said. This resulted in "a very material measure of direct relief to real estate and tangible personal property, which has been bearing an unjust proportion of the burdens of taxation."

During the century between Dillingham's advocacy of the first-ever statewide education property tax and the *Brigham* decision, governors shared a goal of broadened equal education opportunity for students. But their reasons for doing so differed. And how to pay for broader opportunity was an ongoing challenge.

Some governors saw an inability to provide good schooling to all children as a state security issue. Governor Carroll Page said, in 1892, that "with a foreign element pouring in upon us at the rate of 500,000 annually [the national immigration rate in 1892 was actually about 9.5 million[12]], the safety of our institutions will be endangered unless that element can be assimilated . . . . This heterogenous mass can only be made homogeneous by education." If the "second generation" of these immigrants isn't assimilated, Page warned, "we shall be compelled either to maintain a standing army to suppress anarchy, or to close our doors to the emigrants of the world."

Often, the issue of equal education opportunity was seen in rural/urban terms.

Governor John Weeks, in 1929, believed that "the people of Vermont are zealous in their desires to provide for the education of their children." He wanted legislators to "foster the development of our local schools to the end that the children in the rural districts may be given similar advantages to children who are privileged to attend the schools in the larger centers."

The theme of equalizing opportunity was always raised with a caveat, though. In 1931, for example, Governor Wilson noted that "considerable progress has been made in the past few years toward equalizing educational opportunities to the youth of our State." However, he said, "The funds provided for equalizing the cost of education have been insufficient . . . so that as a result the towns have not been getting that which they were promised." Funds should be increased, he said, but that might have to "await a later day."

Two years later, Wilson reiterated the state's commitment to equity of opportunity for children in all schools, rural or urban. But again, there was a qualification: "I feel, however, that our schools are costing us unduly at the present time in many instances. . . . A careful study of existing school laws convinces me that changes can be made that will enable us to reduce expenditures by the state and by the towns without sacrificing efficiency."

Governor George Aiken, in 1937, upon his inauguration, asked legislators to reacquaint themselves with the Vermont Constitution, especially its declaration of rights — "the most progressive political document the New World had yet seen," he said. Noting that changes had been made to state education law two years previously, Aiken advocated no additional changes: "Although we cannot afford to do as much for our schools as we would like to, yet we must be sure that there shall be no let-down to our standards and should strive to improve them at every opportunity."

After the Depression eased and World War II ended, governors gained enough confidence to ask the legislature to do more for the state's children. Governor Mortimer Proctor in 1945 recommended that "the Legislature appropriate sufficient money to equalize the cost of education. . . ." He sought a "higher and a more uniform standard of education."

Governor Ernest Gibson, Jr., seen as a liberal "reform" governor, told legislators in 1947 that the greatest "foundation stones" on which democracy rests are an equal-opportunity school system and sound health. "We reaffirm our belief that education and health are the very foundation stones of democracy and we want to see every Vermont youth at his or her maturity well educated and in good health," he said. In Gibson's view, the greatest problem facing the state's education system was "equalizing educational opportunity and distributing the costs as equally as possible among the towns and school districts of the State." He specifically called for examination of the state's current "equated pupil formula."

For the next fifty years, Vermont struggled with the problems Gibson had identified. The result was a succession of different funding systems — the Miller Formula in 1969, the Morse-Giuliani Formula in 1982, and the Foundation Aid Formula in 1988. The first two — the Miller Formula and the Morse-Giuliani Formula — aimed at equalizing funding across districts through consideration of towns' individual property wealth (Miller) or consideration of both town property wealth and town residents' income (Morse-Giuliani). The third — the Foundation Formula — set a cost per student of an adequate (minimum quality) education and sent "state aid" to towns that couldn't, from their own town's grand list, generate this minimum level of funding at a reasonable tax rate. The system established a floor for poorer communities but still allowed wealthy towns to spend well above the minimum.[13]

Because the bulk of funds came from local property taxes, all these formulas viewed education as a local responsibility, with the state playing a supporting role. Consequently, these "state aid to education" formulas inevitably suffered the same fate: When the state hit hard times and revenues dropped, governors and legislators balanced the state budget by cutting education funds, which produced a downward spiral. With each round of cuts, fewer towns qualified for state aid, so fewer legislators saw a need to support the funding. Towns without much property to tax were hit the hardest, and the gap in per-pupil spending between "property-rich" and "property-poor" communities widened.

Sprinkled among the various funding schemes were school consolidation efforts advocated by the state as cost-saving efficiencies. They were generally opposed by local communities because they would cause loss of local control and local identity. The building of regional high schools and vocational-technical centers was successful, however, when the state's student population began to grow in the 1950s and 1960s and numerous small, local high schools offering limited curricula were seen as inadequate. Local districts were largely left intact, continuing to operate schools in their towns for students in kindergarten through grades six or eight. In 1951, Governor Lee

Emerson noted there seemed "no difficulty on the consolidation of towns in an area for high school purposes," but he opposed the forced consolidation of local districts' elementary schools. He felt that "the determination of the number of schools therein is a matter of local self-government which should be preserved."

The '90s, and forward to equity

The recession of 1990 hit the Foundation Formula particularly hard; state aid to education was one target of the budget cuts that followed the slump. Debates at the State House over school funding reform became perennial, the ferocity growing as political power shifted between Republicans and Democrats in the legislative chambers and the governorship.

Vermont was not alone in its inability to identify and implement a fair school funding formula. Frustration grew around the country when schools in poor rural areas or inner cities were shown to be inferior to those in wealthy suburbs. Increasingly, children's education opportunities seemed to depend on where they lived. Political solutions weren't working, so reform advocates turned to the courts. Hoping to replicate school desegregation victories of the 1950s and 1960s, they looked first to the federal courts. But in a 1973 decision in a case brought in Texas, *San Antonio Independent School District v. Rodríguez,* the U.S. Supreme Court had ruled that the U.S. Constitution doesn't guarantee schoolchildren equal rights to education opportunity. With a federal route to equity blocked, reform advocates turned to state courts. By the early 1990s, lawsuits had been brought in twenty-eight states.[14]

Vermont wasn't yet one of those states. But disappointment in the Vermont legislature's inaction on school funding reform led to continuing speculation about a legal challenge to Vermont's Foundation Formula. Most lawyers were wary of such an endeavor. Challenging a democratically elected legislature's determination of how schools are funded was seen as a tough case to make. The plaintiffs would be up against the full power of the state. Showing harm to communities and their students because of the funding formula would require painstaking statistical analysis. Jurists disagreed on whether the state's constitution could be seen as friendly to such a claim.

If any two people can be identified as setting the *Brigham* challenge in motion in Vermont, it is Ernest Broadwater of Burke and a neighbor, Robert Gensburg. Broadwater was an educator who taught at Lyndon State College. His town's school was struggling to give local children the skills and knowledge he and others believed were needed for success in life. The state's funding system, with its reliance on local property taxes, made raising adequate funds difficult in towns like Burke. Broadwater didn't think that was right, when children attending schools in other, better-funded towns, had more opportunities to learn.

He shared his concerns with his friend, Gensburg, a lawyer who Broadwater knew had a social conscience rooted in the belief that all people should be treated equally under the law. Gensburg told Broadwater he'd think about the issue and whether there might be a way to bring a lawsuit that would result in a fairer education funding system. The result was the filing of the *Brigham* lawsuit in 1995, with the legal support of six other attorneys and the sponsorship of the American Civil Liberties Union of Vermont.[15]

Involving Gensburg signaled that this would be a serious case. He had first gained public notice in the Paul Lawrence drug case of the early 1970s; Gensburg was lead investigator in piecing together how Lawrence, an undercover drug cop, was so successful in busting young people. Lawrence was a fraud, Gensburg determined: He'd planted illegally obtained drugs on his suspects and then arrested them for possession. The story went national.[16]

Gensburg went on to represent organizations providing housing for low- and middle-income Vermonters and, among many other positions, to run a railroad (the result of his serving as the first chair of Vermont's State Transportation Board). Gensburg's commitment to justice was peerless. He also had a mind for figures (his resume included a stint with the National Security Agency as a cryptographer). Toward the end of his life (he died in 2017), he volunteered to represent an Afghan man held as an alleged terrorist at the U.S. military prison in Guantanamo Bay, Cuba. His arrest had been one of mistaken identity, Gensburg showed, and the man was finally freed after fourteen years of imprisonment.[17]

The lawyers who volunteered to work with Gensburg in the *Brigham* case were Victoria Cherney, Joshua Diamond, Frank Kochman, Mitchell Pearl, David Putter, and Peter Welch. All worked pro bono (for no pay). Compensation came in the chance to bring "impact" litigation that could reshape the funding of Vermont public education. Plaintiffs were several school districts, several taxpayers, and several students — one of whom was Amanda Brigham.

The equality sought by the plaintiffs in the *Brigham* case was financial equity — equal access to school funds. This was a strategic decision and a departure from how school equity had been viewed in various funding formulas the state had developed over the years. The

Foundation Formula that was in place when the *Brigham* lawsuit was filed had tried to smooth out the effects of local resource disparities by promising every school district enough money to provide students with a basic education at a reasonable tax rate. If a town wanted to provide more than a basic education, it could do so at its own expense, relying on its own local tax base. This was unfair, Gensburg and his team argued. Property-rich towns could raise additional funds more easily than property-poor towns. Towns should have equal access to school funds.

Such a claim for equal access to financial resources is termed an "equity" education lawsuit, as opposed to an "adequacy" lawsuit, where claims are based on unequal education programs among schools. The *Brigham* lawyers felt that an "equity" claim was better suited to Vermont's constitution.

The lawyers' reasoning turned out to be sound. In its ruling, the Vermont Supreme Court noted that "money is clearly not the only variable affecting educational opportunity, but it is one that government can effectively equalize."

Indeed, the "adequacy" lawsuits brought in a number of other states were ultimately unsuccessful, even if won in court, in bringing about fundamental changes. Failure came because there is no accepted definition of what an "adequate" education is, either in the breadth or the depth of course offerings. In New Hampshire, for example, where an "adequacy" school funding case was brought at about the same time as the *Brigham* "equity" case, agreement on reform has remained elusive despite years of continuing litigation and legislative wrangling. In 2018, a lawyer involved in bringing the original *Claremont School District v. Governor of New Hampshire* case said a new equal education funding lawsuit was needed. The state's response had been inadequate, he said.[18]

The Vermont Supreme Court handed down its ruling in the *Brigham* case on Feb. 5, 1997. In a unanimous decision, the court accepted the plaintiffs' argument that the provision of public education was a state responsibility and that the state constitution's common benefits clause required that it be provided on an equal basis. The opinion held that the education funding system then in place "deprives children of an equal educational opportunity in violation of the Vermont Constitution." The justices acknowledged the tricky relationship between financial inputs and academic outcomes, but they said that "there is no reasonable doubt that substantial funding differences significantly affect opportunities to learn." The justices wanted this to be clearly understood:

> *The distribution of a resource as precious as educational opportunity may not have as its determining force the mere fortuity of a child's residence. It requires no particular constitutional expertise to recognize the capriciousness of such a system.* [19]

The court noted an example of unacceptable disparities. The two towns of Stannard and Sherburne (the latter renamed Killington in 1999) had nearly identical spending per pupil. Yet in Stannard, property taxes on a house valued at $85,000 were $2,040; in Sherburne, taxes on a house of equal value were $247. Such unequal access to funding had to be eliminated, the justices said.

The court soundly rejected the state's argument that the current funding system did enough to equalize opportunities for children. "The State has not provided a persuasive rationale for the undisputed inequities in the current educational funding system," it held. The system is simply "constitutionally deficient." The justices bluntly stated, "Labels aside, we are simply unable to fathom a legitimate governmental purpose to justify the gross inequities in educational opportunities evident from the record."

As it would also do in the *Baker* marriage-rights decision two years later, the court refrained from issuing a judicial solution to the issue at hand. The legislature was the proper place for a solution to be crafted, it said:

> *We acknowledge the conscientious and ongoing efforts of the Legislature to achieve equity in educational financing and intend no intrusion upon its prerogatives to define a system consistent with constitutional requirements. In this context, the Court's duty today is solely to define the impact of the State Constitution on educational funding, not to fashion and impose a solution. The remedy at this juncture properly lies with the Legislature.*

But the court established one baseline mandate that the legislature had to meet: The state must establish a funding system in which "children who live in property-poor districts and children who live in property-rich districts should be afforded a substantially equal opportunity to have access to similar educational revenues." Disparities such as existed between Stannard and Sherburne would not be tolerated.

An important determination in the *Brigham* decision was the court's view that each town should be able to decide for itself how much it would spend on its pupils' education. This determination was the court's acknowledgment of the importance of local control of school budgets.

> *Equal opportunity does not necessarily require precisely equal per-capita expenditures, nor does it necessarily prohibit*

cities and towns from spending more on education if they choose, but it does not allow a system in which educational opportunity is necessarily a function of district wealth.

Protection of local communities' control over their schools took off the table any discussion of exactly which courses schools should or must teach. The result has been that school offerings continue to vary widely around Vermont, particularly among schools of different sizes. This may not seem fair to children, but it is not a constitutional violation. Equality in *Brigham* means equal access to school funds — not equal access to school programs, and not equal student results.

(Local differences in educational offerings, and patterns of lower academic achievement at certain schools or among certain student population groups, became the major focus of the 2015 school-consolidation law, Act 46. While consolidation of town-based districts into larger regional units was required, the core *Brigham* principle of equal access to school funds remained. [One detail of the law – incentives and continuation of small schools grants, even after consolidation – was challenged, unsuccessfully, in court because it seemed to give an unfair financial advantage to towns that accepted merger sooner than other schools.])

From saying what's right to doing what's right

The enormous consequences of the *Brigham* decision were recognized immediately after the court handed down its decision, one month into the 1997 legislative session. A problem that had bedeviled legislators for years now had to be addressed and solved. A new school funding system had to be put in place.

The legislature went into overdrive. Thanks to work done by Representatives Paul Cillo and John Freidin, who had pushed for years to change the education funding system, the House was prepared for the challenge. Committees went right to work retooling the education tax revenue and distribution systems, and developing new accountability standards.

The House Ways and Means Committee proposed creation of a single statewide property tax base. A penny on the tax rate in one town would raise the same amount of revenue per pupil as a penny on the tax rate in any other town. School budgets would still be voted on locally, and towns would continue to make their own decisions about how much to spend on their schools, as the court said they should. A local income tax would be established to ease property taxes. And assessments of property values would be made consistent across the state. But no longer would an individual town's property wealth determine whether it could provide the education programs it wanted for its children. All towns had the same financial base from which to draw.

Meanwhile, broad school quality standards were drawn up by the House Education Committee; these standards included annual local development of action plans charting improvement of a town's school. The two pieces — taxes and general improvement standards — were merged into a single bill, passed, and sent to the Senate.

Senators (and the governor, Howard Dean) didn't like the inclusion of a local income tax in the House bill. The bill went to a committee of conference where the House continued to argue for a local income tax. In the end, a "prebate" system was created that adjusted homeowners' property taxes based on their income. For about two-thirds of Vermonters, their school property tax essentially became an income tax through the prebate "income-sensitivity" program.

Consideration and passage of the bill brought into sharp focus the watershed changes the *Brigham* decision required. Newspapers carried detailed stories about how the law would affect different communities. Letters-to-the-editor pages were jammed with submissions praising and castigating the court decision, the new law, or both. Advocacy groups quickly formed to support or oppose the law. Act 60 (the new law was the sixtieth bill passed and signed into law during the legislative session) became shorthand for education funding reform.[20]

Press attention extended beyond the state's borders. Most of the stories praised the court's decision and heralded the state's bold move to equalize communities' access to school funds in an effort to broaden children's education opportunities. But some stories, focusing on the blending of local town tax bases to create a statewide property tax system, predicted dire consequences.

A story in the Dec. 19, 1997, *New York Times* began, "Vermont these days is riven by revolution."[21] A feature story titled "Don't Tread on My Tax Rate" appeared four months later in the paper's Sunday *Times Magazine* supplement. It quoted a Vermont realtor warning, "I think there will be blood in the streets." The *Times* declared: "The social fabric of Vermont is fraying. The divisions that exist in all societies — between rich and poor, employer and employee, young and old, insiders and outsiders — are widening into chasms." The state was "sinking into a morass of uncertainty, resentment, and recrimination."[22]

It was an ironic observation, given that the law would narrow the gaps that had existed in the funding law.

For me, the issue of equity and education opportunity was personal. I had become involved in the ACLU litigation effort when, as chair of the Worcester School Board, my town's school board agreed to join the *Brigham* lawsuit. I had spent time learning about school funding systems, first as a freelance journalist and then as a school board member when a bond vote to finance an addition to Worcester's overcrowded elementary school was rejected repeatedly by voters. The *Brigham* lawyers saw that I had on-the-ground experience on the issues and encouraged me to prepare to testify as a witness when the case went to trial. (A trial never took place. The case was ultimately litigated on the record produced by the *Brigham* lawyers and the lawyers from the state Attorney General's Office.)

I helped organize a citizens' advocacy group to support the new law. Our president was Phil Hoff, who had served as a representative in the legislature from 1961 to 1963, then as Vermont's governor from 1963 to 1968, and finally as a senator in the legislature from 1983 to 1989. Hoff had a long interest in education equity issues. Also involved was Doug Racine, a former state senator who had been elected lieutenant governor in November 1996.

Money was the chief issue in the debates that followed.

Act 60 clearly delineated the two financial streams of the new law. The first was raising the money to fund Vermont's schools, and the second was distributing the funds to the towns to pay for their schools.

On the distribution side of the funding stream, there was little disagreement. Few opponents of Act 60 — from the harshest critic on down — disagreed with the Vermont Supreme Court's ruling that towns should have equal access to funds for their children's schools.

There was heated disagreement, though, over the question of how to raise the revenue to fund the new system. And this disagreement highlighted a dilemma common to equity issues: A huge political gulf often exists between knowing what is right and doing what is right.

This produces a tension that can be seen as "revolution," as old systems are abandoned and replaced by new ones.

The disagreement around the funding side of Act 60 shouldn't have come as a surprise to anyone. While the court in *Brigham* had spoken with laser clarity on the issue of fairness to kids, it left to the legislature the job of fashioning a revenue-raising system that would be fair to taxpayers. By leaving the solution to the political process, the court tossed legislators into an arena where the predominant question was "Whose ox would be gored?" as participants in the legislative discussions often said.

Interestingly, left on the table in the *Brigham* litigation was another constitutional claim, that of taxpayer equity. This claim was based on Article 9 of Chapter 1 of the Vermont Constitution, which states:

> *That every member of society hath a right to be protected in the enjoyment of life, liberty, and property, and therefore is bound to contribute the member's proportion towards the expence of that protection. . . .*

This so-called "proportional burden" clause has long been eyed by those involved in tax policy questions as an opportunity for the state's supreme court to define fair taxation. The court, however, steered clear of a ruling on this issue in the *Brigham* case. The court said the issue hadn't been adequately briefed by the state. This meant that further consideration of the claim would require additional litigation. The case would need to return to the trial court level, a prospect that neither side viewed with enthusiasm.

When, in June 1997, Act 60 became law, the parties agreed to drop any further claims and to ask the court to close the case. A determination of what constitutes "proportional burden" was left to another day.

From the plaintiffs' perspective, a major victory for schoolchildren had already been won. It did not appear tactically wise to draw things out any further.

(In 2001, Bob Gensburg was asked to speak to new legislators about the *Brigham* lawsuit — its background and the resulting legislation that had been passed to meet the Vermont Supreme Court's order to restructure the state's education funding system. During testimony before the House Ways and Means Committee, Gensburg noted the unresolved claim brought under Article 9. He told the committee, "I would like to say that, in my opinion, the outcome of another lawsuit if something like that ever happened, in my opinion is a foregone conclusion. And I think that it would say that article 9 prohibits a taxation system that has disparities of five and six and seven and eight times the amount of taxes paid to support this state [education] function." The disparity rates noted by Gensburg referred to differences in school property taxes paid by residents of different towns under the previous Foundation Formula, the school funding system found unconstitutional in the *Brigham* case.) [23]

It would have been interesting to see the "proportional burden" issue fully litigated. Tax fairness questions are constantly raised, and not just about school taxes. It's hard to guess where the court may have landed on an important question that would presumably have affected not just property taxes but all forms of state taxes.

That Act 60 has lasted more than twenty years (the law's twentieth anniversary was noted at a State House event in February 2017) is testimony to the fact that, while the funding system created in the law may not be perfect, it is better than others. National education policy experts rate Vermont's system one of the fairest in the country.[24]

While the equity of the revenue-distribution side of Act 60 has been widely accepted, there is a perception among critics of the law that homeowners whose property taxes are adjusted according to their income, rather than based solely on the value of their property, aren't paying their fair share. Perceptions can be difficult to unravel, especially when there's an undeniable truth underlying the issue. In this case and others around taxation, the truth is that no one likes paying taxes. Add to that truth the complexity in Act 60 of prebates, rebates, income-sensitivity, equalized pupils, and spending per pupil, and people begin to believe the system can't possibly be working as promised.

The relevant truth underlying perceptions of fairness may lie in the object being taxed for schools: property. Someone's home may not be as good a measure of wealth today as it was two hundred, one hundred, or even fifty years ago. Property taxes are also regressive; the amount paid is typically a larger share of income for poor or middle-income families than for wealthy families. Some people think it might be time to base all school taxes on income rather than the value of people's homes. But others insist we should stick with tax tradition and keep property as the basis for school taxes. The property tax is a more stable source of revenue than the income tax, they say, especially during economic downturns.

In reporting that Vermont was "riven by revolution," *The New York Times* may have been right in one respect. A major change had occurred in the state. The change came in the way that Vermonters were asked to think about children's education. They were asked to extend their vision for kids' schooling beyond their individual towns to the entire state. They were asked to take on a sense of collective responsibility to guarantee equal access for all children to the fundamental right of public education.

'Our reputation as a fair-minded state is at stake'

The late Vermont poet David Budbill — who tangled with another Vermont author, John Irving, over the changes to school funding — put it this way:

> Beyond all the arguments about how Act 60 will be implemented, there is a fundamental question: Do we as a people here in Vermont believe our children, all our children, no matter where they come from or how rich or poor they are, deserve an equal opportunity for an education? Our reputation as a fair-minded state is at stake. And so is the future of our children.[25]

The funding equity brought about by the *Brigham* decision — far-reaching as it was — has increasingly been viewed as not sufficient in making education opportunities for children fully equal. That belief is based on differences in the range of courses offered at small schools vs. large schools and on test results showing children from lower-income families consistently scoring below children from middle- and upper-income families. Financial equity as an input, in other words, hasn't always translated into equity of school curricula or equity of student performance as outputs.

This raises the question, What exactly is fairness when it comes to education? Is equal access to school funds a worthy goal in and of itself? Or must it be considered one step on a path toward a broader goal of ensuring all children have an equal chance to succeed in life through equal opportunities provided by public education? If the latter is the case, what elements must be present for such success to be available to all children?

In a sense, achieving school funding equity may face the same difficulty as defining an "adequate" educational program. Equity of funding is undoubtedly important, but it may only be a piece of ensuring that all children have the opportunity to become happy, caring, productive adults who are involved in the lives of their communities. It's good, but not enough.

The number of variables that play a part in a child's development is vast. Some variables are certainly due to resources — resources such as money and the creation of specific education programs, for example — that can be equalized by government. But other variables are affected by things beyond community or state control. Strong families, positive role models, parents who care about learning, friends or mentors who guide a child in developing positive interactions with others — these are all things that can greatly influence a child's success in school and in later life but can't be mandated by a court and supplied by government. Education researchers believe that many factors leading to a child's success in school lie outside of a school's control: Parents' education, economic circumstances, and social standing may carry more weight than the instruction a child receives in the classroom.[26]

Indeed, education is perhaps one of the most challenging tasks a government can undertake. The formation of common schools two hundred years ago in America was the result of a belief that democratic society has an important stake in how children grow up. We believe our society demands training that consumes a considerable number of years in one's life as well as significant expenditures by taxpayers. It's a public investment in the country's future.

There is no perfect education system — or, if there is, after hundreds of years of trying, we haven't yet found it. Schools can always improve, and the challenge in ensuring that meaningful improvements are made is listening to those criticisms that speak to the core mission of schools rather than expressing a temporary disappointment because of societal changes or local circumstances.

Increasingly, public education officials and advocates in Vermont worry that the state's schools are beginning to reflect the general economic and social stratification occurring within American society at large.[27] The original purpose of the Vermont legislature's Act 46 school consolidation law passed in 2015 may have been to change the organization of school districts to save money, but the focus of the final product was on "school quality" and expanded opportunities for students. (Within a year of passage of Act 46, legislative supporters acknowledged that little money would be saved.)

Rebecca Holcombe, the state's education secretary at the time that Act 46 was passed, used the phrase "school dependent" as shorthand for those children who depend on schools, rather than their families, for basic needs such as food, safety, shelter, and nurturing. The inequality of circumstance (such as family wages, housing, or health care) that has become a central theme in American political debates is present in the nation's school systems as well, including Vermont's.

And as in other parts of the country, citizens and public education officials in Vermont have begun to worry that advocates of private schools and school choice point to the large number of society's problems that schools are now asked to address as a reason to privatize education or to create charter schools that may have restrictive enrollment policies. Such an alternative, others feel, will result in increased inequality of opportunity.

In 2015, former *Washington Post* reporter Dale Russakoff wrote *The Prize,* an exhaustively researched book on Newark, N.J., school reform. In the early 2000s, then–Newark Mayor Cory Booker, a Democrat, and New Jersey Governor Chris Christie, a Republican, formed an unlikely alliance to remake Newark schools through intervention by private education consultants and charter school advocates. The effort received more than $100 million from high-flying tech executives such as Mark Zuckerberg of Facebook and Wall Street financiers. Russakoff, who lived in New Jersey, grew curious about how the money was being spent and how the residents of Newark felt about the closing of numerous neighborhood schools and the creation of new magnet and charter schools.[28]

I didn't think there were many connections between issues facing Newark schools and those facing Vermont schools until a hearing at the Vermont State House in the fall of 2015. I was struck by testimony given by some Vermont school officials regarding tensions in their communities.

The purpose of the hearing was to gauge how well implementation of Act 46 was proceeding, specifically towns' compliance with the school consolidation requirements. As educators spoke, their descriptions of what they saw in their schools in Vermont sounded eerily similar to descriptions offered by Russakoff in her book about Newark schools. Substitute place names, and much of Russakoff's narrative could apply to Vermont. The inequality of circumstances in which children are growing up is largely the same.

Russakoff wrote of the challenges facing the Newark school superintendent, Cami Anderson:

> *Surprisingly, Cerf [Christopher Cerf, a former New York City school reformer appointed New Jersey education commissioner in 2010], Booker, and Christie . . . couldn't answer*

Anderson's questions: How many district schools will have to close? Where will displaced children go if there is no longer a school within walking distance? (With its long history of neighborhood schools, Newark did not provide school busing.) How will district teachers address an increasing concentration of children with emotional and learning challenges? Had anyone calculated a sustainable size for a diminished Newark district? In shaking up the bureaucracy, reformers said often that they were prioritizing children's education over adult jobs. But in their zeal to disrupt the old, failed system, many of them neglected to acknowledge the disruption they were going to cause in the lives of tens of thousands of children.[29]

Dorinne Dorfman, who was then the principal of Leland & Gray High School in Townshend in southern Vermont, traveled to Montpelier for the November 2015 hearing before the House Education Committee. She told legislators that one of the towns in her union high school district

is especially vulnerable to widening socioeconomic inequalities as a result of redistricting and school choice. Research on school choice in Vermont as well as Leland and Gray's own demographic trends demonstrate that students and parents select schools based on social class, with more affluent families choosing those in higher-income areas.

Citing various education policy experts, Dorfman elaborated:

Over a decade of state testing has not closed the achievement gap. Instead, poverty and mental illness have grown. Without thoughtful analysis, population redistribution in schools and supervisory districts can tip the scales and create high con-centrations of disadvantaged students that reduce advanced programs, increase costs, lower school achievement, and dim students' futures.[30]

Dorfman's union high school district was struggling. Her message to lawmakers was clear: A top-down approach from Montpelier that dictated what's best for children could easily limit, rather than expand, education opportunities for students who need help the most. It's what Russakoff showed was happening in Newark.

We have come to think of our schools as the means by which the adversity of personal circumstance is erased, children thrive, and, with the education they receive, join people of different ethnicities, races, genders, sexual preferences, religions, and abilities and live successful, fulfilling lives in harmonious communities.

We expect thirteen years of education (with perhaps two or three years of preschool as well) to overcome our country's long history of uncomfortable realities such as warfare against Native Peoples, racial subjugation, economic division, ethnic and gender discrimination, and religious parochialism. We have built our democratic country at a high cost — which we continue to pay through stratification, inequality, and marginalization of many groups and classes of people.

Astounding, perhaps even humbling, is that many Americans still say that they believe in equality. The reality of our history, layered on a polyglot society operating through a complicated government, can be seen as suggesting that equality can't be achieved. Yet we continue to strive toward it, a small state like Vermont unafraid to assert that "equal" really does mean "equal."

The arc of the moral universe is long, the abolitionist Theodore Parker said in 1853, but "it bends toward justice."[31] If there is a simple definition of justice, it is that all are treated equally. The common benefits clause of the Vermont Constitution is perhaps best seen as a weight that tries to increase the bend of morality's arc so we move more quickly toward justice and equality. Changing the state's education funding formula may not bring equality immediately, but it does help to bend the curve — and that, to the state's credit, is a significant achievement.

Chapter 2

Marriage Equality

Within only a few years of the U.S. Supreme Court's 2015 Obergefell v. Hodges *decision legalizing same-sex marriages, gay marriages began to seem ordinary and commonplace. Millennials, especially, wondered, What's the big deal? Why did it take so long?*

The gay rights struggle began in the states. Vermont was a crucial battlefield in this struggle. In a ground-breaking 1999 decision, Baker v. State, *the Vermont Supreme Court ruled that same-sex couples had the same right to marriage benefits as did opposite-sex couples. The court's decision let the Vermont legislature decide how to provide those benefits — through marriage or something else. The legislature chose the "something else" option — "civil unions." Gay couples would have the benefits of marriage without being married.*

Civil unions appeared an innovative solution, but critics said it was no different than the "separate but equal" approach used to discriminate against African-Americans. "Jim Crow" laws persisted for more than a century before they were overturned during the civil rights movement of the 1950s and 1960s. The Vermont legislature (although not the governor at the time) came around to this thinking, and, in 2009, civil unions were tossed out in favor of marriage for gay and straight couples alike. Discrimination based on sexual orientation seemed a thing of the past.

But in 2010, two women approached the ACLU. They had been told they couldn't hold their wedding reception at a scenic inn near Burke Mountain in the Northeast Kingdom. The innkeepers said that their "personal feelings precluded them from allowing such events at their property." The couple wanted to know, "Can they do that?" I was executive director of the ACLU in Vermont at the time. ACLU lawyers were pretty sure the answer was "well, not legally," but we knew we'd have to go to court to make the innkeepers accept that as fact. A national religious rights organization had agreed to help the innkeepers mount a vigorous defense of what they saw as a right to discriminate. A court battle ensued, a bitter legal fight that spilled over into the national press. The couple, Kate Baker and Ming Linsley, were disconsolate.

Kate and Ming came to Montpelier in July 2011 for a press conference announcing the filing of the lawsuit. The event took place in Room 10 in the State House. The easiest way to direct someone to that room in the capitol building is to tell them to meet by the Lincoln statue on the first floor. A large bust of Abraham Lincoln is right outside the entrance to the room. Kate and Ming had no trouble finding it. We reviewed the protocol for the press conference and then talked informally. I wanted to know how they had decided to undertake the lawsuit; it was clear, chatting with them, that this had not been an easy, or comfortable, decision to make.

"I think I was just struck by the injustice of it and feeling it's so hard to not take that kind of thing personally and not feel in some way that you're being told by society that whoever you are is unacceptable or inappropriate or not wanted," Ming said.

The lawsuit moved forward. Eventually, the couple prevailed —
although the inn's owners then decided there would be no receptions
for any couples, straight or gay, at their property.

The case, and the gay rights struggle over many years, reminded
me of two observations that advocates point to regarding civil
rights issues:

1. The candid answer to someone's question, "Can they do that?" when
   their rights have been violated, is almost always yes — because the
   harmful action has already occurred. The pertinent question is,
   "Can the offenders get away with the violation?" Organizations like
   the ACLU work, often through lawsuits in court, to ensure people
   can't get away with violating others' rights.

2. Veterans of civil rights battles smile, albeit wearily, when someone
   complains how long vindication can take when you must go to court
   to win your rights. The founder of the ACLU, Roger Baldwin, used
   to say, "No fight for civil liberties ever stays won." Rights must
   constantly be fought for and protected, or they will disappear.

Gay rights advocates in Vermont showed how persistence and
vigilance can overcome centuries of discrimination.

"We didn't bring the lawsuit to punish the Wildflower Inn or to
collect money," Ming said when their legal fight was over. "We brought
this lawsuit because we wanted people to understand that what the
Wildflower Inn did was illegal. We didn't want to stay quiet and allow
businesses to continue to discriminate against other couples."

Shortly after the Wildflower case closed, the Lincoln statue in
the State House was cleaned. It had gotten grimy since it was erected
in 1912. The 150th anniversary of Lincoln's Gettysburg Address
was approaching, and historians wanted the statue to shine. It did.

Lincoln looked brighter. For me, the shine was like a knowing smile from a weary advocate that yet another battle for justice had been won by two determined individuals who chose not to be silent.

•

The road to the *Baker* decision

The Vermont Supreme Court's decision in the case of *Baker v. State* was big news not just in Vermont but nationally and even abroad when it was announced in December 1999, a few days before the new millennium. The decision was the first time in the United States that a court had ruled that same-sex couples were entitled to the same benefits heterosexual couples receive through marriage.

The decision was based on the guarantee of equity provided by Article 7, the common benefits clause of the Vermont Constitution — the same clause on which the court had decided the *Brigham* case two years earlier.

Support for gay Vermonters' rights had been building through the 1990s. Vermont was one of the first states to adopt a hate crimes law (in 1990) that included protections for gay men and women. In 1992, "sexual orientation" was added as a "protected class" to the state's antidiscrimination law. A 1993 court case upheld the rights of same-sex partners to adopt children. In 1994, Vermont granted health insurance benefits to domestic partners (including gay partners) of state workers, the first state to do so.

Nationally, there was a burst of hope for marriage equality when, in 1993, the Hawaii Supreme Court ordered the state to show a compelling reason why gay couples couldn't marry. However, a successful state ballot initiative outlawing gay marriage made a response moot. The Hawaii court's original inquiry, though, energized gay rights advocates around the country to consider court challenges of marriage laws as a route to equality.

In 1995, the Vermont Coalition for Lesbian and Gay Rights began looking closely at the marriage issue. Two lawyers, Beth Robinson and Susan Murray, were part of a committee that developed materials to train advocates to talk about same-sex marriage. A new organization, the Vermont Freedom to Marry Task Force, spun off from the Coalition's work, with Robinson and Murray its leaders. The Task Force mounted a statewide education campaign to introduce the issue to the public, with members appearing at county fairs and numerous public and private venues. Their presentations were straightforward, often personal, and compelling on a level of basic humanity.[32]

A number of gay and lesbian couples contacted Robinson and Murray about getting involved in same-sex marriage litigation. Three emerged to become the plaintiff couples in the *Baker* case, filed in 1997 — Stan Baker and Peter Harrigan, Holly Puterbaugh and Lois Farnham, and Nina Beck and Stacy Jolles. Joining Robinson and Murray as the plaintiffs' attorneys was Mary Bonauto of Gay & Lesbian Advocates and Defenders (GLAD), a national gay rights advocacy organization based in Boston.

The *Baker* decision was written by Chief Justice Jeffrey Amestoy. Amestoy had been appointed by Governor Howard Dean in 1997 to replace retiring Chief Justice Frederick Allen. Amestoy had been state attorney general, elected to that position as a Republican in 1984 and re-elected six times. He was an affable, well-known presence in Montpelier who, when not doing legal work, loved to talk about baseball and Patrick O'Brian sea novels.

Amestoy was not Dean's pick for the important chief justice position. William Sorrell, Dean's administration secretary, was. Dean's preference for Sorrell was seen as payment of a political debt to the Sorrells, a prominent Burlington family active in Democratic Party politics. Esther Sorrell, William's mother, had encouraged and supported the young Howard Dean as he had shifted his career from medicine to politics in the 1980s. But a judicial screening committee didn't include Sorrell on its nomination list of capable candidates; Amestoy was on it, though. Dean acquiesced to Amestoy's appointment, and then awarded Sorrell the attorney general position that Amestoy vacated.

Each appointment was crucial in its own way. Sorrell went on to win election to the attorney general's office for a total of nine terms, more than any other Vermont attorney general. Amestoy's appointment as chief justice added new energy to the court, which became apparent through the *Baker* decision. It is hard to imagine Sorrell's writing such a historically rich, persuasive document. Indeed, the attorney general's office under Sorrell led a vigorous defense of the status quo (as, it should be pointed out in fairness, was the duty of the attorney general's office to do).

Amestoy's opinion in *Baker* is clear and direct. That he was the identified author of the opinion stands in contrast to the *Brigham* decision, which had no identified author or authors (*Brigham* carries only a general per curiam — for the court — attribution). Amestoy was the second-newest member of the court at the time and had had no experience as a judge. The court's system for assigning opinions was random; it wasn't the chief justice's decision. In the end, though, the chief justice's authorship likely lent an air of gravitas to the opinion — and displayed Amestoy's deep interest in, and understanding of, history.[33]

After framing the marriage issue in the opinion's first paragraph, Amestoy delivered the conclusion that the court had reached unanimously: The common benefits clause entitled same-sex couples to the same marriage rights granted opposite-sex couples.

This was a huge victory for LGBTQ (lesbian, gay, bisexual, transgender, and queer) advocates. The Vermont Supreme Court could not have said more precisely and succinctly that same-sex couples cannot be treated differently from opposite-sex couples when it comes to marriage's "benefits and protections."

But there was a caveat — and it was a huge disappointment to the plaintiffs and to gay rights advocates nationally. While gay couples were entitled to marriage's "benefits and protections," the court said they weren't necessarily entitled to "marriage" itself:

> *Whether this [the extension of marriage benefits] ultimately takes the form of inclusion within the marriage laws themselves or a parallel "domestic partnership" system or some equivalent statutory alternative, rests with the Legislature. Whatever system is chosen, however, must conform with the constitutional imperative to afford all Vermonters the common benefit, protection, and security of the law.*

The immediate impact of the *Baker* decision was to encourage the Vermont legislature to move deliberately but quickly — despite the intense emotion around the issue — to meet the court's mandate. By March, after long discussions in the House Judiciary Committee chaired by Representative Thomas Little, and contentious, emotional testimony at public hearings, the House passed a bill and sent it to the Senate. The bill created a parallel route, "civil unions," to marriage's benefits. The Senate, after another round of contentious discussions

and hearings, concurred, and Governor Dean signed the bill into law —
privately, with no ceremony, and with no photo to mark the occasion
and no signing pens for supporters. (This stood in stark contrast to the
governor's signing of Act 60 in June 1997, the legislature's response to
the *Brigham* decision. That signing was at a public celebration at plaintiff Amanda Brigham's elementary school in Whiting, outside, under
blue skies, with reporters and photographers chronicling the event.)[34]

Looking back, Dean's closet signing of the civil unions bill was
a portent of what was in store for the *Baker* decision. As the years
passed, the decision was shunned by national gay rights advocates. The Vermont Supreme Court, the advocates said, had given
permission to the state's legislature to create something less than
marriage for gay couples. It amounted to second-class citizenship; civil
unions were not equal to marriage, they said. Advocates continued
to push, in state after state, toward full marriage equality. The
Massachusetts Supreme Judicial Court was the first state court, in
2004, to rule that "marriage" as a legal institution could not be sepa-
rated from its benefits and protections; they were a package. Even
after Vermont became the first state, in 2009, to mandate marriage
through legislative action, its one-time leadership in the march to
marriage equality became, for many people outside Vermont, a historical footnote.

(At a national ACLU conference in 2013, the *Windsor v. United
States* gay rights case taken by the ACLU to the U.S. Supreme Court
was being analyzed. Hoping for a victory in *Windsor* — which did
come, two weeks after the conference — presenters recounted the
road to marriage equality. One speaker termed Vermont's civil unions
law a mere "booby prize" on that road, an embarrassing half step that
showed a lack of courage. Sitting next to me at the conference was

one of the justices from the *Baker* court; the justice remained wooden through the presentation. I felt empty.)

Within Vermont, the view on the *Baker* decision was, and remains, that it was historic, that people have forgotten or glossed over the depths of anti-gay sentiment at the time, and that the public conversation that ensued through the Vermont legislature's discussions after *Baker* paved the way — dangerously rocky at first — toward widespread acceptance of a major cultural, social, and, to many, moral shift in the treatment of members of the LGBTQ community. A marker noting the decision and subsequent changes in Vermont marriage laws was erected in 2017 on the lawn between the State House and the supreme court building, the only such marker near the two buildings that commemorates a specific political or historical event.

The difficulties on the road Vermont traveled, between the initial euphoria that greeted the *Baker* decision in 1999 and its nudge by others to history's wayside, were many. Feelings against both Act 60 and the civil unions law ran high during the 2000 fall campaign. Incumbent Governor Howard Dean, running for re-election, was advised by his security detail to wear a bulletproof vest when campaigning in public.[35] Large "Take Back Vermont" signs appeared on garages and barns around the state. The signs — handmade, the stark black letters painted on a 4 x 8 sheet of plywood — stood out in a state that doesn't allow billboards.[36] A raft of highly respected legislators who had supported civil unions lost their seats. One, Richard Mallory, a former Republican with a distinguished political career that included service as speaker of the Vermont House and member of Congress, had returned to the House in 1999 as an independent. Another, Marion Milne, a House Republican from Washington, Vermont, ran one of the state's largest travel bureaus; she felt strongly about public service and had served four terms in the legislature. "If I am measured only by this one vote in my entire public life," she said, "I have served my constituents well by voting for this bill."

Dean won re-election as governor, but Republicans gained control of the Vermont House of Representatives (although not the Senate). Howard Dean's departure from Vermont politics two years later to begin a national campaign for the presidency allowed Republican James Douglas to move in to the governor's office in 2002; he remained there for eight years. Whereas Dean didn't block civil unions, Douglas steadfastly opposed gay marriage. When the legislature passed the marriage equality bill in 2009, he vetoed it. The Democrats, then in control of both chambers, mustered the necessary votes for an override. The House vote was as narrow as possible — opponents could have sustained the governor's veto had they been able to flip just one legislator.

That the state's Republican Party — the party of Lincoln that established equality before the law through the Fourteenth Amendment — would stand on an anti-equality platform was, to some, a turning away from basic principles of fairness. Mallary, in an interview shortly before his death in 2011, said he voted his conscience on the gay marriage bill in the belief that the Republican Party that he knew stood for principles "of equal rights, justice, and opportunity for all."[37]

We agree, but . . .

Lost in the testy politics that surrounded the *Baker* decision was the justices' lengthy questioning of how the state's common benefits clause should be applied in future cases of alleged discrimination and inequality. Thumbing through the forty-four-page decision, one finds that more pages deal with future application of the state's common benefits clause than with gay rights.

This discussion within a discussion is a window onto why some claims to equity under the Vermont Constitution have succeeded and why future claims are likely to face formidable, but by no means insurmountable, odds.

At the root of the issue of future applicability of the common benefits clause are these two questions: Who is entitled to equality? and, Equality of what?

Technically, the *Baker* decision was unanimous, 5-0. But to Amestoy's opinion, two justices appended separate opinions — a way of saying, "We agree, but . . . "

Justice John Dooley, in a concurring opinion, agreed with the view that same-sex couples are entitled to the same benefits of marriage as opposite-sex couples, but he disagreed with the way the common benefits clause was being applied to reach that conclusion.

Justice Denise Johnson, in a concurring and dissenting opinion, agreed with the other justices on the equal marriage rights determination and shared Dooley's concern about the way the common benefits clause was being applied. But what most concerned Johnson was the remedy provided by the court — a charge to the legislature to find a solution to the denial of marriage rights. Johnson felt strongly that the court's duty when a right is violated is to restore the right as quickly as possible. Officials empowered to conduct weddings should be ordered to grant marriage licenses to same-sex couples, she said: the view that the legislature was best able to figure out how to deliver equality was an abrogation of justice. "Absent 'compelling' reasons that dictate otherwise, it is not only the prerogative but the duty of courts to provide prompt relief for violations of individual civil rights," Johnson wrote.

Johnson disagreed with what the other justices deemed strategically necessary — an extensive public conversation undertaken in the legislature on acceptance, through changes to the state's statutes, of equal marriage rights. This was ironic. In the *Brigham* case just two years before, the court provided the constitutional framework for school funding equity, but it declined the role of implementer. Johnson had approved of this approach in the *Brigham* decision, but she vehemently disagreed with it in *Baker*. "Passing this case on to the Legislature will not alleviate the instability and uncertainty that the majority seeks to avoid," she wrote.

The press and public didn't spend much time discussing the disagreements arising from the concurring opinions, other than to draw a breath at Johnson's strong admonition to the court that it wasn't doing its job. Everyone's focus was instead on where the Vermont Supreme Court had landed in regard to whether gay couples could marry. There was little said about what, in the long run of history, could prove to be the deeper significance of the *Baker* decision: the court's discussion of where the common benefits clause could take the state when citizens press for greater equity in any of a number of areas.

Many court decisions dwell extensively on process (for example, whether rules of evidence and procedure are followed, or standards applied correctly); but they usually also spend a complementary amount of space — if not more — on the issue specific to the case at hand. However, of the twenty-two pages in the main *Baker* opinion (the part written by Chief Justice Amestoy), only about seven focus on what marriage is and why its benefits and protections are important, no matter whether a couple is straight or gay. The other fifteen pages concern legal process. In the twenty-two pages of the two concurring opinions, it's the same pattern: Only seven focus on marriage while the remaining fifteen address legal process. All told, fourteen of the total forty-four pages of the three opinions are about marriage, and thirty are devoted to the legal process used in applying the protections of the common benefits clause.

The legal process issues discussed in the concurring opinions include dire pictures of how judges, because of the majority's opinion, will struggle in the future to deal with equity cases. Were one to employ layman's language, "It'll be a mess" might be the most succinct way to describe the predictions.

Amestoy's majority opinion held that questions of equality brought in Vermont courts under the state constitution's common benefits clause should be judged by standards different from those applied to questions of equality brought in federal courts under the Fourteenth Amendment to the U.S. Constitution. The standards used in federal courts to evaluate the constitutionality of government actions ("strict scrutiny," "intermediate scrutiny," and "rational basis" standards) don't suffice for interpreting the demands of Vermont's common benefits clause, Amestoy wrote.

Jettisoning the federal standards (which are relatively objective, in legal terms) and replacing them with a more Vermont-specific subjective analysis worried Justices Dooley and Johnson. The court will be forced to dig deeper into the dimensions of the equity that Vermont's founders sought when they wrote Article 7, the two justices said.

A history lesson on equity and the principle of inclusion

That seems to be exactly what Amestoy hoped would happen. Indeed, a good deal of his majority opinion is a history lesson on how equity was viewed by Vermont's founders and how that should affect how we view discrimination — and how we can eliminate it — today.

Amestoy asked that we think about the meaning of equity when the state was founded and apply that understanding in deciding whether today's government is treating the state's citizens fairly. He himself seemed to relish this challenge. "We turn, accordingly, to a brief examination of constitutional language and history," he wrote, almost as a teacher might begin a lecture before an eager class.

He pointed to the many factors — a "shifting and complicated kaleidoscope of events, social forces, and ideas" — that led to the inclusion of the common benefits language, first in the Pennsylvania Constitution and then in the Vermont Constitution. He said that the words themselves of the common benefits clause are "revealing." He wrote:

> While they do not, to be sure, set forth a fully formed standard of analysis for determining the constitutionality of a given statute, they do express broad principles which usefully inform that analysis. Chief among these is the principle of inclusion. As explained more fully in the discussion that follows, the specific proscription against governmental favoritism toward not only groups or "set[s] of men," but also toward any particular "family" or "single man," underscores the framers' resentment of political preference of any kind. The affirma-

tive right to the "common benefits and protections" of govern-
ment and the corollary proscription of favoritism in the dis-
tribution of public "emoluments and advantages" reflect the
framers' overarching objective "not only that everyone enjoy
equality before the law or have an equal voice in government
but also that everyone have an equal share in the fruits of the
common enterprise." Thus, at its core the Common Benefits
Clause expressed a vision of government that afforded every
Vermonter its benefit and protection and provided no Ver-
monter particular advantage....

The exploration of Vermont political and social history goes on,
something unexpected in a court ruling about same-sex marriage.
Amestoy pulls in quotations from well-known American historians
to explain the evolution of key principles in the nation's history. The
detail creates an urgency to understand our past. This may sound like
a lesson in political science, but one can almost hear Amestoy saying,
"This is important. This matters to us today":

Although aimed at Great Britain, the American Revolu-
tion — as numerous historians have noted — also tapped
deep-seated domestic antagonisms. The planter elite in
Virginia, the proprietors of Eastern Pennsylvania, and New
Yorkers claiming Vermont lands were each the object of
long-standing grievances. Indeed, the revolt against Great
Britain unleashed what one historian, speaking of Penn-
sylvania, has called "a revolution within a revolution." By
attempting to claim equal rights for Americans against
the English, regardless of birthright or social status, "even
the most aristocratic of southern Whig planters . . . were

pushed into creating an egalitarian ideology that could be and even as early as 1776 was being turned against themselves." While not opposed to the concept of a social elite, the framers of the first state constitutions believed that it should consist of a "natural aristocracy" of talent, rather than an entrenched clique favored by birth or social connections. As the preeminent historian [Bernard Bailyn] of the ideological origins of the Revolution explained, "while 'equality before the law' was a commonplace of the time, 'equality without respect to the dignity of the persons concerned' was not; [the Revolution's] emphasis on social equivalence was significant." Thus, while the framers' "egalitarian ideology" conspicuously excluded many oppressed people of the eighteenth century — including African-Americans, Native Americans, and women — it did nevertheless represent a genuine social revolt pitting republican ideals of "virtue," or talent and merit, against a perceived aristocracy of privilege both abroad and at home.

Amestoy noted specific conflicts in Vermont at the time. "Vermont was not immune to the disruptive forces unleashed by the Revolution," he wrote:

One historian has described Vermont on the eve of the Revolution as rife with "factional rivalry [and] regional jealousy." Competing factions in the Champlain and Upper Connecticut River Valleys had long vied for political and economic dominance.... another historian has spoken of "Vermont's double revolution — a rebellion within a rebellion" to describe the successful revolt against both Great Britain and New York

by the yeoman farmers, small-scale proprietors, and mod-
erate land speculators who comprised the bulk of the Green
Mountain Boys.

Just when a reader might be wondering what exactly discussion of eighteenth-century American social and political conflicts might have to do with legal definitions of equality, Amestoy tells us that from this ferment emerged a constitution considered by some to be the country's most democratic:

The powerful movement for "social equivalence" unleashed
by the Revolution ultimately found its most complete expres-
sion in the first state constitutions adopted in the early years
of the rebellion. In Pennsylvania, where social antagonisms
were most acute, the result was a fundamental charter that
has been described as "the most radical constitution of the
Revolution." Yet the Pennsylvania Constitution's egalitarian-
ism was arguably eclipsed the following year by the Vermont
Constitution of 1777. In addition to the commitment to gov-
ernment for the "common benefit, protection, and security,"
it contained novel provisions abolishing slavery, eliminating
property qualifications for voting, and calling for the gover-
nor, lieutenant governor, and twelve councilors to be elected
by the people rather than appointed by the legislature. These
and other provisions have led one historian to observe that
Vermont's first charter was the "most democratic constitution
produced by any of the American states."

Amestoy pointed out that the equality Vermont's founders were discussing wasn't quite what we might think of today. The framers were "enlightened for their day," he said, but they "were not principally concerned with civil rights for African-Americans and other minorities." Instead, the Vermont founders' focus was on "equal access to public benefits and protections for the community as a whole. . . . The Vermont Constitution would ensure that the law uniformly afforded every Vermonter its benefit, protection, and security so that social and political preeminence would reflect differences of capacity, disposition, and virtue, rather than governmental favor and privilege."

This distinction is important. The concept of equality as seen by the state's founders in 1777 aimed at defining a core sense of equity among all citizens. This is different from the concept of equality in the U.S. Constitution's Fourteenth Amendment. That "equal protection" amendment, passed in the wake of the defeat of the Confederate states in the Civil War, aimed at rectifying unequal treatment of African-Americans.

This core sense of equity means that the scope of Vermont's common benefits clause is broader than the scope of the equal protection clause of the U.S. Constitution. The Vermont Constitution establishes a principle of "inclusion," Amestoy said. "Article 7 is intended to ensure that the benefits and protections conferred by the state are for the common benefit of the community."

It's the concept of an "inclusionary principle" that must guide the analysis of discrimination cases brought under the common benefits clause of the Vermont Constitution, Amestoy wrote. He admitted that this approach might be seen as more subjective than following the standards used in federal courts, but he suggested specific factors that can be used to determine when discrimination is occurring:

> *We must ultimately ascertain whether the omission of a part of the community from the benefit, protection and security of*

the challenged law bears a reasonable and just relation to the governmental purpose. Consistent with the core presumption of inclusion, factors to be considered in this determination may include: (1) the significance of the benefits and protections of the challenged law; (2) whether the omission of members of the community from the benefits and protections of the challenged law promotes the government's stated goals; and (3) whether the classification is significantly underinclusive or overinclusive.

The court's determination can be kept "grounded and objective, and not based upon the private sensitivities or values of individual judges" through assessment of "the relative weights of competing interests," Amestoy said. Citing language from a 1961 U.S. Supreme Court case, *Poe v. Ullman,* he said "courts must look to the history and traditions from which [the State] developed as well as those from which it broke, and not to merely personal notions." (The *Poe v. Ullman* case concerned the prohibition of contraceptives by the state of Connecticut.)[38]

In the end, "reasoned judgment" is the key to a fair evaluation of constitutional claims brought to the court under the common benefits clause, Amestoy wrote:

The balance between individual liberty and organized society which courts are continually called upon to weigh does not lend itself to the precision of a scale. It is, indeed, a recognition of the imprecision of "reasoned judgment" that compels both judicial restraint and respect for tradition in constitutional interpretation.

This line of reasoning is what Dooley challenged in his opinion. He worried that judges' "identities and personal philosophies" rather than "ascertainable standards" would be used when deciding cases brought under the common benefits clause.

"The final irony in this decision for me," said Dooley,

> is that the balancing and weighing process set forth in the Court's opinion describes exactly the process we would expect legislators to go through if they were facing the question before us free from the political pressures necessarily created by deeply held moral convictions, in both directions, of substantial members of their constituents. We are judges, not legislators.

Amestoy foresaw an intellectually energetic court assessing the strengths of competing claims. Dooley feared Amestoy's approach would lead to excessive court activism in reviewing economic and social welfare legislation.

This rift showed an important struggle. The court, through Amestoy's opinion and the two dissenting opinions, was grappling with how this powerful judicial engine it was sparking to life could best — and most fairly — be harnessed in the future. The justices wanted to establish a road map. It was hard to do. In a footnote, Amestoy conceded as much — but said the challenge was a good thing:

> Characterizing a case as affecting "economic" interests, "civil rights," "fundamental" rights, or "suspect classes" — as our colleagues apparently prefer — is no less an exercise in judgment. Indeed, it may disguise the court's value judgments with a label, rather than explain its reasoning in terms that the public and the litigants are entitled to understand.

Pragmatic constitutionalism

Amestoy's *Baker* opinion may have frustrated some of his fellow justices and disappointed marriage equality advocates. Legislators may have wished the court had provided more specific guidance on how best to revise marriage rights statutes to make them constitutional. But Amestoy was seeking a longer vision about how Vermonters can best use the equality protection of the state constitution's common benefits clause.

The chief justice's opinion caught the attention of jurists interested in state constitutional law.

Since 1988, the law school at Rutgers University in New Jersey had published an annual issue of the *Rutgers Law Journal* that focused on state constitutional law — the sort of law, Vermont Supreme Court Justice Hayes had said in his 1985 *State v. Jewett* opinion, that could "protect the rights and liberties of our people, however the philosophy of the United States Supreme Court may ebb and flow."

The journal's 2004 edition included a lecture written by Amestoy called "Pragmatic Constitutionalism — Reflections on State Constitutional Theory and Same-Sex Marriage Claims." In the lecture, Amestoy referenced a theory of "state constitutionalism" proposed four years earlier by Professor Douglas Reed of Georgetown University in an article also published in the *Rutgers Law Journal*. Reed's theory was that the "processes of generating state constitutional meanings . . . are subject to much more intense political disputation by interests and coalitions of interests than is the Federal Constitution."[39]

The *Baker* decision was handed down shortly before Reed's article went to press. Reed added a footnote about the decision, noting the court had not mandated a specific solution to ensuring gay couples had marriage rights equal to those of heterosexual couples. Reed wrote that the Vermont court had recognized that "a decision which mandated same-sex marriage outright might face intense opposition." He quoted this sentence from the Baker decision: "[I]t cannot be doubted that judicial authority is not ultimate authority." And then Reed stated, "That, in a nutshell, is the lesson of popular constitutionalism."[40]

Amestoy wrote in his 2004 article that many of Reed's insights were, indeed, relevant to the *Baker* decision. But he also noted an observation in G. Alan Tarr's 1998 book, *Understanding State Constitutions,* that "no one theory of state constitutional interpretation explains the evolution of the New Judicial Federalism." Amestoy suggested that the *Baker* decision reflected what he thought of as "pragmatic constitutionalism." As an analogy of what courts must sometimes do, Amestoy talked of building a house and having to modify it from time to time to suit the needs of its inhabitants.[41]

At the root of pragmatic constitutionalism, Amestoy said, was recognition that courts may not always have the "right" answer in responding to issues fraught with sharp political edges. "In state constitutionalism," Amestoy wrote, "*both* law and politics matter."[42] He then noted an observation made by Professor Cass R. Sunstein that was quoted in the *Baker* decision:

> "When a democracy is in moral flux, courts may not have the best or the final answers. Judicial answers may be wrong. They may be counterproductive even if they are right. Courts do best by proceeding in a way that is catalytic rather than preclusive, and that is closely attuned to the fact that courts are participants in the system of democratic deliberation."[43]

Amestoy described how a court can become part of the democratic deliberation:

If one accepts — and I understand that there are those who do not — the premise that sound state constitutionalism must acknowledge that judicial authority is not ultimate authority, then a paramount objective of a judicial opinion must be persuasiveness. By "persuasive" in this context, I mean more than the analytic rigor and sound legal reasoning that one should expect from a competent appellate court engaged in state constitutional interpretation. And I mean something other than a contribution one hopes a state constitutional opinion like Baker *may make to a national dialogue about equality. The opinion must in its use of history, text, analysis, and language resonate with those who — to return to my architectural analogy — live in the house and have the power to alter it.*[44]

At the end of his article, Amestoy looked back on what had happened after the *Baker* opinion was issued. His observation ended with a reference to a Longfellow poem that speaks of "one family only, one heart, one hearth, and one household" — equality, in other words:

Whatever Baker*'s ultimate fate as a statement of independent state constitutional jurisprudence, the experience of the Vermont community in responding to the opinion does demonstrate, I believe, that by conscious choice of language and analytic structure, a state appellate court may either arrest or advance the public debate even in such highly charged issues as same-sex marriage.*

. . . In concluding that extending the benefits and protections of marriage to the plaintiffs was "simply, when all is said

and done, a recognition of our common humanity," the Baker *opinion was intended to resonate with* every *Vermonter. For in our constitutional system,* every *Vermonter is a participant and we all live in the same house. We will know we have built well when — in the words of the poet — "underneath that roof there was no distinction of persons, but one family only, one heart, one hearth, and one household."* [45]

The real achievement of the *Baker* decision may be to show Vermonters that the state's common benefits clause is based on enlightened thinking from 250 years ago and that the clause really *does* mean that the benefits a society offers its citizens must be provided on an equal basis. Just because a benefit or right isn't specifically mentioned in the state constitution doesn't mean it's disqualified for review under the state's common benefits clause.

Such an approach would be radical — which perhaps is precisely what the state's founders hoped the common benefits clause would encourage and what Amestoy felt it should, with the court's help. Using the common benefits clause to create such equity might not be easy. But perhaps the full bravery of the *Baker* decision, and of the common benefits clause, is yet to be tapped

Chapter 3

Health Care Reform

D eb Richter is a fearsome ball of energy. She's a primary care doctor from Montpelier with a practice in Cambridge. She sees, on a daily basis, the ill effects of a health care system that's expensive and doesn't cover everyone. "Dr. Deb," as some of her patients call her, has fought since the 1990s for health care reform. Her core belief is simple: Everyone is entitled to affordable medical care. She has served on innumerable health care reform committees in Vermont and nationally. She testifies often before the state legislature. She writes op-eds and sends letters to local papers. She exudes a four-square commitment to publicly financed universal health care coverage. She'll never give up the fight.

In 1999, Deb contacted me. She knew of my involvement in the Brigham *lawsuit.* "How can we do for health care what's been done for education funding?" she asked. "Can the legal approach used in Brigham *be utilized to bring a lawsuit mandating equal health care access for all citizens?"*

We met at a picnic table outside the Champlain Mill in Winooski, where I was working at the time. I told her my understanding was that a constitutional approach wouldn't succeed for health care reform.

But I agreed to arrange a meeting with the lead Brigham *attorney, Bob Gensburg, to discuss the idea. That meeting resulted in the same conclusion — there appeared to be no constitutional lever to move health care reform forward. Health care isn't mentioned in the state or federal constitutions, and the health care laws that have been enacted over the years don't suggest a right of equal access for all citizens.*

I had the sense that Deb had expected that response, yet it was one more branch she felt she had to shake. Health care reform in Vermont has been that way. For nearly a hundred years, Vermonters have shaken many branches and suggested many ideas, but the goal of affordable health care for all has remained elusive.

A different kind of equity claim is at play in health care compared to education and marriage rights. It is its own fight, but equity is still the goal. In joining the host of Vermonters who have labored to reach that goal, Deb Richter has pushed us closer to where we know we should be — but haven't yet figured out how to get there.

•

A doctor-governor tries for reform

Lieutenant Governor Howard Dean was hard at work at his regular job of family doctor when he got an urgent phone call on a summer day in 1991. He interrupted his physical exam of a patient to take the call. He was told that earlier that morning, Governor Richard Snelling had a massive heart attack and died. Dean was now governor. He needed to get to Montpelier right away to assume his new duties.

While Dean was seen as ambitious, no one guessed he'd land in the state's top office so quickly. But from the start of his unforeseen ascension, he seemed to relish the job. He had developed a list of initiatives while running for lieutenant governor in 1990, so his general interests were known. But few guessed how quickly he'd move on one of those interests — health care reform.

Within a year, the "doctor-governor," as he was sometimes called, saw the legislature approve a bill sponsored by Democratic House Speaker Ralph Wright to have the state's newly created Health Care Authority study the state's health care system. The Authority's mandate was to develop a choice of plans to create what was termed a "universal health care" system that would provide health coverage to all Vermonters. One of those options had to be a single-payer plan. (In a single-payer system, only one entity — usually the government — handles payments, which is much more efficient and saves money when contrasted to a system in which numerous private insurance companies sell policies and process claims.) The requirement that a single-payer option be developed was the result of strong efforts by two members of the state Senate, Senators Sally Conrad and Cheryl Rivers, to move Vermont toward adoption of a single-payer health care system. They had introduced a single-payer bill in 1991, had held hearings in their committees and around the state, and by 1992 were picking up key endorsements for the bill from labor and human rights organizations.

Two years later, in 1994, Speaker Wright stood before his party's House caucus at the start of the week when a comprehensive reform bill — the outcome of the Authority's work — would be taken up. The previous week, Wright had counted eighty-eight votes in favor of a "sweeping 'single-payer' system," a dozen more than needed for House passage. Wright himself wasn't wedded to the plan, and Dean was felt to be lukewarm-to-cool on single-payer. What both wanted, though, was universal coverage. It seemed they should at least be able to get that, with such a margin willing to reach for the even tougher goal of single-payer.

Wright was worried, though. He would later write in his autobiography, *All Politics is Personal,* "Things weren't looking very good for the issue that we had put so much of our time and energy into over the past two years and we were barely hanging on to the smallest semblance of the revolutionary measure that had struck such excitement in our hearts two years earlier. Time, cost, and complexity of the issue had been our greatest enemy."[46]

Joining those three opposing forces — time, cost, and complexity — to create Wright's pre-vote jitters were lurking critics such as Harry and Louise. Harry and Louise were two middle-aged, middle-class TV citizens scripted in a national ad campaign launched in 1993 to undermine the national health care initiative of newly inaugurated President Bill Clinton.

President Clinton's plan was shaped by his wife, Hillary Rodham Clinton, whom he had appointed chair of a presidential task force on health care. Howard Dean had become a high-profile supporter of the Clinton effort, sitting behind Ms. Clinton in the gallery of the House Chamber in the U.S. Capitol when President Clinton described his health care plan to a joint session of Congress. Hopes were high that finally the United States would join other developed nations and establish a national health care system for all citizens.

But the Clinton plan unraveled during a bruising fight that, among other things, spawned a deep-seated animosity between the Clintons and conservatives, an animosity that would persist for the next quarter century.

The Vermont plan championed by Dean suffered collateral damage from the national angst over comprehensive reform. Between the Wednesday of the week when Wright had taken his head count showing eighty-eight House members in favor of a universal single-payer plan and the Tuesday of the pre-vote caucus, opponents had "pulled out all the stops realizing Vermont just might be small enough, even innocent enough, to do the right thing and provide a universal health plan for all its citizens," Wright related in his autobiography.

The Democrats had to admit, Wright said, that "we were David without the slingshot." Member after member came up to him, or his legislative health care point person, Representative Sean Campbell, and said they could no longer support a shift to a state-run universal health plan. It — and not just the single-payer element — was too radical.

Seeing that he no longer held the votes to pass the plan, Wright settled for a watered-down version and the hope that he and the governor could revive a universal coverage plan in the Senate. "I never dreamed of giving up," Wright said. "It wasn't in me. Besides, we still might pull it all together, for even though we didn't have a majority of Democrats in the Senate, the public demand still seemed to be there, and we had the doctor/governor who had gotten this whole thing started."

It wasn't to be.

"We were ten thousand feet above New Jersey when the end came," Wright explained.

He and Dean were flying to Washington for a political fundraiser. Dean was calmly reading *The New York Times*. Wright turned to him and said, "'Governor, what are we going to do with the Health Care Plan in the Senate?'"

Wright noted Dean's response in one sentence. "He barely looked up from his reading and he nonchalantly answered, 'Nothing, it's dead.'"

Two years later, when Wright penned his book, he was still fuming over Dean's airplane death pronouncement. He wrote rhetorically, "That's it? It's dead? Two years of grinding and fighting and it's dead? Everything went out of my mind, as the only visual I had was the Governor in a hospital room, pulling another sheet up over a patient's face, and turning to look at the charts on the patient in the next bed."[47]

The same story would play out twenty years later, albeit on the ground in a much more public space. Another governor would pronounce another comprehensive health care reform effort — one based on a single-payer model — dead. But instead of a distraught House speaker mourning defeat in the solitude of an airplane high above New Jersey, this time an angry coalition of advocates would shut down formal legislative proceedings at the State House, drawing the ire of legislators.

Shumlin promises he'll deliver

The Vermont State House is a genteel place; shutting down business there crosses a line of what's viewed as acceptable behavior.

For their part, the advocates acted as they did because they felt betrayed. In 2010, in his first gubernatorial campaign (which featured a bruising five-way primary election and a razor-thin general election), Democrat Peter Shumlin had promised creation of a single-payer, universal-access health care system. Single-payer advocates, working since the Conrad-Rivers bill of 1991, cheered; they believed Vermont was finally nearing a victory many had thought impossible to achieve after so many years of stalled efforts.

After his 2010 election, Shumlin got to work immediately on his agenda, with health care at the top of his list. In the first legislative session of his tenure, the Democratic legislature passed a comprehensive bill that created an independent health care regulatory board, the "Green Mountain Care Board." The law, Act 48, assigned the board three main areas of responsibility: regulation (of hospital budgets, major health care projects, and health insurance rates); innovation (changes to payment processes, review of the state's health care workforce plan, and oversight of the build-out of the state's electronic medical records exchange system); and evaluation (of the state's current health care system and of the development of a new health care system to be called "Green Mountain Care"). Anya Rader Wallack, a veteran of health care reform efforts and well-respected in New England health care circles, was chosen to lead the five-member Green Mountain Care Board. The board plunged into its work.[48]

A visit by Harvard economist William Hsiao stoked the enthusiasm for comprehensive reform. Hsiao, an internationally known health care finance expert and once chief actuary for Medicare and Medicaid, was familiar with health care systems around the world. He had recently designed a single-payer universal-access system for Taiwan. Along with Jonathan Gruber, an MIT economist who specialized in modeling health care systems, and Steven Kappel, a Vermont data analyst, Hsiao had been contracted by the Shumlin administration to examine how the state could provide comprehensive, affordable health insurance for all Vermonters. As with the 1991 legislation, options were to be provided, one of them a single-payer model. Hsiao acknowledged the challenge of such reform, but the basic message from the group was, "Vermont can do this."

An article in the Harvard University student newspaper, the *Harvard Crimson,* profiling Hsiao and his work, said that all eyes were on Vermont:

Now, advocates for a single-payer system hope that Vermont can serve as a model during future efforts to reform the health care system on either the state or federal level. If so, Hsiao's work will be on center stage.

Given the amount of gridlock and partisan rancor on Capitol Hill, Hsiao says that the only hope at widespread reform may be on the state level. Though reform in Vermont is still early in the implementation process, experts predict that if it succeeds, the state would likely become an example for other larger states to follow. California, Oregon, Pennsylvania, Minnesota, and Colorado have all approached Hsiao in recent months to solicit his help in possible reform efforts in their states.

Robert J. Blendon, a professor of health policy and politics at the Harvard School of Public Health, where Hsiao taught, said Hsiao was, without a doubt, the person who could make single-payer work in Vermont. "If I was a country or a state and I wanted to set up a public health care system, he's the guy I would call," Blendon said. "He's just one of the best in the world."[49]

High hopes. But in December 2014, Shumlin decided it wasn't to be. After three years of study and extensive modeling, his administration couldn't get single-payer — the plan the governor had promised — to work. The money just wasn't there, Shumlin said. Efforts would continue on specific, smaller pieces of health care reform, but building a system where everybody was in and everybody was guaranteed care through a publicly financed system was not going to happen.

The announcement of the (second) death of single-payer, and of protestors' State House disruption, were overwhelming evidence that Shumlin couldn't keep his promises. He saw where his dropping of the health care ball had landed him. In July 2015, he announced he wouldn't run for re-election in 2016.

One governor's pulling the plug on health care reform in 1994, another in 2014: Despite the interest and energy around the health care issue, nothing seemed to have changed in twenty years.

Not Vermont's first attempts at health care reform

The truth is, Vermont has a century-long record of disappointment when it comes to health care reform. Starting in the 1920s, the state has looked at many changes to improve medical services for Vermonters in a way they can afford. No one has been satisfied with the overall results, although many incremental improvements have been made.

Former state archivist Gregory Sanford once undertook an effort to locate articles on health care issues in Vermont newspapers from the 1920s and 1930s. He found that, in October 1930, *The Burlington Free Press* editorialized about the "Saskatchewan plan," which had begun in 1921 and encouraged towns in the western Canadian province to hire doctors to provide affordable care to local residents. (Saskatchewan would go on to establish a province-wide public health system in 1962, leading the way to Canada's nationwide health insurance system in 1968. The architect of the system, Tommy Douglas, is seen by Canadians as a national hero.)

In a 1931 report, the Vermont Commission on Country Life recommended the state adopt the Saskatchewan plan. Each town would hire a doctor (salaries of $2,800 for part-time and $5,000 for full-time doctors) to provide free treatment to families within the municipality.

Sanford noted that while the Vermont Legislature didn't adopt the Saskatchewan plan, some towns went ahead anyhow and took it upon themselves to try to improve care in their communities. The national Committee on the Costs of Medical Care, which "spent several summers in Burlington in the early 1930s" studying health care access and cost, found that in some Vermont towns "subsidies are paid to physicians out of tax funds . . . making them accessible to citizens in the locality."

Other initiatives were tried, Sanford found. He noted that, in 1930, for instance:

> Stowe voted to provide "eyeglasses for school children whose parents are unable to meet the cost." The same year Richford voted $175 as a milk fund for school children whose parents are unable to meet the cost, while Thetford appropriated $227.50 for the services of a Red Cross nurse in the schools. Chelsea and Strafford voted $500 to encourage doctors to locate in their communities, while Arlington, Sunderland, Poultney, and Rockingham proposed $1,000 incentives to attract doctors or nurses.

Sanford discovered that Brattleboro Memorial Hospital had even set up what amounted to a major medical services insurance plan for town residents.[50]

In 1944, the Vermont Rural Policy Committee issued a report, "Rural Health After the War." Tellingly, World War II itself had revealed the state's health care challenges — thirty percent of Vermont draftees had been rejected for military service because of poor health. County committees identified specific issues and brainstormed solutions: There was a need for services for returning soldiers, mental health and dental health, wellness programs, and even "socialized medicine, hospital insurance, and health care for all." The subcommittee that had been charged with sketching a "social security program for rural Vermont" stated, "Regardless of their economic status our men, women, and children must be assured medical, nursing, and hospital attention."

The committee grappled with "finding a balance between cooperative and socialized medicine," Sanford said.

> *The committee recognized that a third of Vermonters could not afford regular health care. It expressed its belief that "it is an important part of our program to educate the people to accept the principle that society should assume a part of the financial responsibility for the physical and mental well-being of its citizenry, and to cooperate with a health program, and further consider the public nature of the program, not on a basis of charity (either by those who receive the benefits and/or those who contribute), but to accept these as we do our educational system, namely, any money used on health is not an expense, but a good investment."*[51]

On the national level, President Franklin Roosevelt's administration looked broadly at the nation's health care needs in the 1930s (at the same time that Social Security was established) but decided a national health care program was too far a reach. FDR didn't lose interest in the issue, though. In his fourth campaign for president in 1944, he outlined an "Economic Bill of Rights" that included a "right to adequate medical care and the opportunity to achieve and enjoy good health."[52] Little action would be taken on health care while World War II continued.

In April 1945, FDR died in office of a massive stroke. Harry Truman, FDR's successor, picked up the baton of reform and included national health insurance in his "Fair Deal" proposal of 1949.

The belief in the power of government to do good through massive change was losing strength, however, and opposition to what some termed "socialized medicine" was fierce. When Ben Turoff, an old friend of Truman's, wrote him a letter criticizing his plan, Truman responded:

> *I can't understand the rabid approach of the American Medical Association — they have distorted and misrepresented the whole program so that it will be necessary for me to go out and tell the people just exactly what we are asking for . . . .* [53]

Truman eventually had to drop his health insurance plan. There were apparently more Ben Turoffs than the president realized.

Truman's successor, Republican Dwight Eisenhower, had little interest in health care reform. But Lyndon Johnson, when he succeeded to the presidency upon John Kennedy's assassination in 1963 and then when he was elected in his own right in 1964, made broadened health care coverage part of his "Great Society" social program. Within seven months of his election, Johnson won approval in Congress for Medicare and Medicaid. It wasn't coverage for all citizens, but it was the nation's largest expansion ever of government-financed health care.

The success of these two programs, despite vociferous opposition from Truman's nemesis, the American Medical Association, kept interest for broader reform alive through the 1970s and 1980s. While Medicare remained a system for seniors, Medicaid's original scope — health care for the disabled poor — grew in some states as federal matching dollars were used to start programs for children and uninsured low-income Americans.

That's what happened in Vermont when interest on the federal level for health care reform remained barely lukewarm. Governor Madeleine Kunin, for example, used Medicaid funds in 1988 to expand coverage for children through a new program called "Dr. Dynasaur." It was the state's first effort to provide health care for those not otherwise covered by insurance plans.[54]

The Dr. Dynasaur program came in the context of an effort that had started in Vermont in the late 1970s to broaden health coverage. Underlying any expansion, however, was a recognized need to control costs. And how to control costs required a better understanding of the state's health care system and how it operated.

Such an understanding began, in 1979, when the state started requiring hospitals and other major health care facilities to obtain a "certificate of need" (CON) before making new capital expenditures or adding new services. The establishment of this CON process was an attempt to control costs and spend precious resources wisely. Richard Snelling was governor at the time. He was a Republican. His support for the CON law showed that, in Vermont, health care reform wasn't a partisan issue, as it had become on the national level.

In 1983, a new entity, called the Hospital Data Council, was created to try to achieve greater efficiencies. The five members of the council reviewed budgets of each of the state's hospitals on an annual basis, suggesting ways costs could be controlled. In doing this work, the council collected comprehensive information about hospital costs and services, and so-called "utilization data" that showed the demand for various health services. Policymakers finally were able to develop a clearer sense of what the state's health care "system" was and how exactly it operated.

Another important development in Vermont's effort to broaden health care access came in 1991, when the legislature passed a law requiring health insurance companies to use "community rating" when accepting patients into their plans. For-profit insurers often showed a preference for selling policies to certain populations (such as younger people, or people without "pre-existing" medical conditions) who generally needed less care. The practice, referred to as "cherry picking," offered greater profit margins for insurers through reduced claims.

The legislature's insistence on community rating was a strong signal that the state's ultimate goal was health care for all. Indeed, that same year, 1991, Governor Snelling had appointed the blue ribbon commission whose charge was "to explore and design a comprehensive group of proposals" to, among other things, ensure "access to adequate health care for all Vermonters." Governor Dean became the one to deal with the commission's recommendations following Snelling's death in August of that year — recommendations that ultimately hit a wall in the 1994 debacle described earlier.[55]

Dean then followed Kunin's lead in tapping Medicaid funds to broaden health care services for specific populations. After Dean left office in 2003 and was replaced by Republican Jim Douglas, incremental change continued. A Blueprint for Health was developed to improve services for the chronically ill. The Catamount Health program, which offered income-based subsidies so uninsured Vermonters could buy health insurance, followed. Structural changes in the health care finance system, such as payment reform (how doctors are paid for the services they provide), moved forward.

Health care as a human right

The dream of a single-payer universal access system (what devoted advocates consider the holy grail of health care reform) was kept alive by these successes. But there was a flip side to the gains: They highlighted the gaps that still existed. That was what had prompted Shumlin in 2010, when he first ran for governor, to promise voters he'd complete the transformation of Vermont's health care system so that everyone would be covered and costly inefficiencies eliminated through a single-payer system.

For Shumlin and the single-payer advocates who believed his campaign promises, memory of the stumbles of previous universal, publicly funded reforms had dimmed or been forgotten.

It was impossible in 2010 for progressive reformers not to feel supercharged about tackling big public-policy changes. To have been in Vermont when the *Brigham* decision was handed down, Act 60 passed, and the state education funding system overhauled, and when, after *Baker,* gay rights advocates worked tirelessly, step by step, to win first civil unions and then marriage equality — these were heady times that few citizens of any state ever get to experience. Vermonters saw that government could be made to bring about monumental, principled change, despite intense opposition and major obstacles.

The State House protests in 2015 following Shumlin's retreat from his single-payer promise were organized by the Workers' Center, an energetic advocacy group based in Burlington. The Workers' Center had adopted health care reform as its singular focus. The group's advocacy campaign was based on a national model for change titled "Health care is a human right." This assertion struck a lofty tone. If schoolchildren had a right to equal education resources, and gay couples had a right to marriage, certainly all people should have a right to health care.

In the abstract, the assertion is hard to refute. After all, the United Nations' "Universal Declaration of Human Rights," adopted in 1948, includes access to health care as one of the basic rights of all citizens of all nations. But in an American court, an assertion of a right in international law doesn't constitute a valid legal claim upon which a successful lawsuit for denial of a right can be based. Both the *Brigham* and *Baker* lawsuits were based on state constitutional protections. No such protection for health care access has yet been found in either the Vermont or U.S. constitutions. Health care may be considered a basic human right *in theory,* and it may be good public policy. But without the benefit of a constitutional mandate, it's not something that can be taken to the legal bank, so to speak.

When I became ACLU-VT executive director in 2004, I received other queries similar to that of Deb Richter in 1999. I again asked Bob Gensburg, and other lawyers who had been involved in constitutional challenges concerning a number of issues, for their opinions on the likelihood of succeeding in a lawsuit based on a constitutional claim of equal access to health care. They all felt the same: There was little chance of winning such a suit. I contacted lawyers outside Vermont, and I received the same answer: A constitutional claim that government must provide all citizens with health care was unlikely to succeed.

The implicit message was that Vermonters had to fight for equal health care access without the weapon that had won *Brigham* and *Baker.* Health care equity requires a different battle strategy.

The tack the Workers' Center advocates tried — "health care is a human right" — was certainly a creative approach. While the strategy failed to achieve advocates' stated goal, postmortems of the campaign pointed to a number of wins in terms of changing minds and focusing attention on health care issues. Health care changes have continued, albeit on a much smaller scale than reformers once hoped.

(There is only one group of citizens that has been found to have a constitutional right to health care — prisoners. In the case *Estelle v. Gamble,* decided in 1976, the U.S. Supreme Court found that the U.S. Constitution's Eighth Amendment prohibition against cruel and unusual punishment was violated because of inadequate medical care that Texas inmate J.W. Gamble had received. Gamble was injured in an accident while he was on a prison work assignment — a six-hundred-pound bale of cotton fell on him. Despite intense pain, he received nothing but pills from doctors. He sued the state of Texas in a handwritten, twenty-four-page complaint, representing himself in what's called pro se litigation. Justice Thurgood Marshall, the author of the 8–1 majority opinion in the case, wrote that "deliberate indifference to serious medical needs of prisoners" violated Eighth Amendment rights. The decision is cited today in most lawsuits over inadequate medical treatment of inmates.[56])

Where is Tommy Douglas?

Why has the fight over universal health care been so long and so hard? Why hasn't someone found the lever that can push things over the top? Where is Vermont's — or for that matter, America's — Tommy Douglas, the Canadian health care hero?

Vermonters, as well as most Americans, acknowledge that something is terribly wrong with the U.S. health care system. We know we spend more per capita than other countries for care that doesn't produce commensurately better results.[57]

What, then, prevents us from moving beyond agreement that "we have a problem" and creating a new system that works better for everyone? Is there such a deep-rooted aversion in America to government involvement in social welfare issues that we're supposed to appreciate that we have Medicare and Medicaid and leave things at that?

Perhaps there is something unique about health care that makes reform of medical services so difficult. Medical needs are individual. Some people get cancer or need a hip replacement, and others don't. Even if you get prostate or breast cancer, there's a question of whether expensive surgeries are justified. And instead of replacing a hip, maybe you should just get a walking cane, take ibuprofen, and deal with the pain.

And then there's mental health, with causes and conditions that can be elusive, and treatments that are still being identified. Should the same level of care — so-called "parity" — be provided for mental health conditions as for physiological conditions?

What about dental and vision care? They're hardly ever mentioned in discussions of health care needs. Don't they deserve parity, too?

Is it these financial complications, individual decisions about pain, care, treatment protocols, convenience, and other complex and value-laden decisions that make us distrust a health care system that would extend a basket of benefits to everyone? Is this where our notion of equity stops? We don't trust each other to take only what we need? And we act this way even though there is ample evidence that we could all be getting much more health care for the money we spend?

With single-payer (again) dead in Vermont, a new health care holy grail has been identified — ACOs, or accountable care organizations.

In 2016, the state's Green Mountain Care Board approved two pilot projects to see if shifting the health care system's focus from paying doctors for the number of procedures they perform to paying them for keeping people healthy can improve medical services and save money.

The strategy behind setting up ACOs is achieving incremental change through the use of incentives. It is not a fundamental restructuring of health care financing or a broadening of coverage to all, such as a single-payer universal-access model seeks. Insurance companies are not eliminated, and only a portion of patients — mainly those in Medicare and Medicaid — were included in the pilot projects. Vermont is, to a great extent, playing the role of niche innovator to try to continue to move forward in the fraught universe of health care reform.

After the Green Mountain Care Board's approval of the ACO pilots (branded as "OneCare"), national news media picked up on the initiative and trumpeted its potential promise. "This tiny state, with a population more rural and less diverse than the country as a whole, is embarking on an experiment that could transform the delivery of health care nationwide," wrote former *Baltimore Sun* reporter Michael Ollove.[58]

In Ollove's story, improving patient care at lower cost was the headlined goal of the OneCare pilots. There wasn't a breath about universal access or a publicly financed single-payer system.

Will ACOs be the silver bullet supporters promise? Some observers, including those tasked with monitoring success toward Vermont's goal of affordable health care for all, are worried. In comments submitted November 2018 to the Green Mountain Care Board, the Office of Health Care Advocate stated that "OneCare's activities and 2019 budget proposal do not meaningfully address Vermont's health care Affordability Crisis." The Office's chief health care advocate,

Michael Fisher — who once, as representative from Ripton, chaired the House Health Care Committee — warned that providers may benefit from the ACO approach while insurance costs to patients continue to rise at unsustainable rates. "Vermonters and the Vermont economy cannot afford to continue on this health insurance rate trajectory," he said. The intricacies of the payment systems, in other words, could allow hospital costs to stabilize at a sustainable rate while insurance rates or other costs to patients continue to rise dramatically.[59]

Whether all Vermonters should be able to get the health care they need at a price they can afford — the notion of health care as a right — remains a question still looking for an answer. Improving health care services and saving money for providers are laudable goals — but should a state whose constitutional core rests on equity for its citizens be satisfied with these goals alone? For all practical purposes, the concept of health care equity appeared to have been left on the table following Governor Shumlin's abandonment of his reform initiative in 2014.

Why are we not in the same boat when it comes to health care?

Vermont is described by many people as a small state that's really more like a large community. People pitch in to help a neighbor and step up when there's a natural disaster like a flood. If you go off the road in the winter, more than likely someone in a pickup truck with a tow rope or chain will stop and pull you out. Is this willingness to act on a sense of "we're all in this together" a critical element that enables Vermont to take on and succeed in tackling big issues, too, such as school funding and marriage equality? If so, why has this element of collaborative effort not extended to health care reform?

Whenever I reach this point in wrestling with which human needs are considered so basic that we establish legal mechanisms to ensure no one can be denied access to them, I think of the sentence in a footnote of Chief Justice Jeffrey Amestoy's *Baker* opinion. It relates to the scope of the Vermont Constitution's common benefits clause:

> *[A]t its core the Common Benefits Clause expressed a vision of government that afforded every Vermonter its benefit and protection and provided no Vermonter particular advantage. . . .*

In two instances in the last twenty-five years, this vision has been turned into reality. With health care, it remains an aspiration.

Acknowledgement of aspiration rather than reality makes one ache when reading the dedication in a report published in 2001 by Vermont's Commission on the Public's Health Care Values and Priorities. The commission had been created in 1994 through a resolution shepherded through the legislature by Representative Karen Kitzmiller after the failure of the Dean-Wright reform plan. Kitzmiller had concluded that legislative efforts were not moving health care reform forward. At the very least, the resolution read, "a process should be designed and implemented to engage Vermonters in a dialogue about values and priorities in Vermont's health care system." The commission members were ten people from diverse advocacy groups and two legislators.[60]

"Hard Choices," the commission's first report, in 1996, discussed the results of a survey of four hundred Vermonters who had been asked about their values and priorities around health care.

The legislature did not respond with a new health care reform initiative. Kitzmiller was undeterred; she kept pushing the issue.

And then she, herself, developed a serious illness and became a patient within the state's health care system. She was diagnosed with metastatic breast cancer, from which she died in 2001.

The report that the commission published that year, shortly after Kitzmiller's death, was dedicated to her. It was designed as a primer to the system that had served her. It was called "Understanding Health Care: An Introduction to Vermont's Health Care System." The commission acknowledged that the report was only "scratching the surface." But, the commission members said, "We hope to give you enough information to help you understand what kind of decisions need to be made so that we can have a health care system in Vermont that meets the needs of all people, at a cost that everyone can afford."[61]

Few descriptions of what health care equity means are so succinct — "a system that meets the needs of all people at a cost everyone can afford." And with such a clear vision, it's hard to accept that in a state that prizes equity, we still haven't built a publicly financed health care system that delivers universal coverage.

While our state constitution's common benefits clause may not be deemed applicable to health care, the founders' inclusion of such a provision in our core political document is a reminder to Vermonters of a responsibility to consider the importance of equal access to society's benefits. A society's strength is built on inclusion, a sense that we're all in this together and everyone counts. Equity is not a partisan ideology in Vermont. It's a foundational value, embedded in our constitution. No other state holds as strong a vision of the need for citizens to work together in a way that ensures fairness and equity.

Calvin Coolidge, as flinty as the rock on which his birthplace of Plymouth Notch rests, expressed this view in a speech he gave in 1925 in Omaha, Nebraska, to an American Legion gathering:

[W]hether one traces his Americanism back three centuries to the Mayflower, or three years of the steerage, is not half so important as whether his Americanism of to-day is real and genuine. No matter by what various crafts we came here, we are all now in the same boat."[62]

When it comes to health care, we're discovering that we're actually not all in the same boat. Instead, because of the complex, twisted financial webs that blur differences between "profit" and "nonprofit" medical enterprises and the sheer scale of medical services, we're in a flotilla of different boats, moving in different ways and offering different classes of passage. We haven't figured out how to build one big ship of one class to accommodate us all — or discovered a method of engaging our constitutional system to force its construction.

Reflecting on the 2016 presidential election, Elizabeth Kolbert, a writer for *The New Yorker* magazine, probed a question that arose among voters who had backed the loser: How is it that reasonable-seeming people are often totally irrational?

Kolbert turned, for an answer, to a book published in 2017 by two cognitive scientists — Hugo Mercier, who worked at a French research institute in Lyon, and Dan Sperber, who was based at Central European University in Budapest.

Mercier and Sperber argued that "humans' biggest advantage over other species is our ability to cooperate." And, they wrote, "Reason is an adaptation to the hypersocial niche humans have evolved for themselves." In other words, reason is the grease that helps us mesh together, to cooperate with one another. That doesn't guarantee, however, that cooperation is easy, Kolbert noted:

Cooperation is difficult to establish and almost as difficult to sustain. For any individual, freeloading is always the best course of action. Reason developed not to enable us to solve abstract, logical problems or even to help us draw conclusions from unfamiliar data; rather, it developed to resolve the problems posed by living in collaborative groups.[63]

Perhaps, then, the Vermont Constitution's vision of equity, created through equal access to society's privileges and benefits, should be seen as the application of reason to bring about collaboration — an ability that sets us apart from other animals. Striving toward equity becomes one of the most important goals for a society hoping to work together to accomplish more than individuals working alone can. As Kolbert wrote, for an individual, "freeloading is always the best course of action." But for a group hoping to achieve more, recognizing the value of collaboration is the appropriate course of action.

Compared to most other states, Vermont has done well in collaborating to improve health care. The incremental changes made over nearly a century demonstrate remarkable progress. But there is still work to do. Health care access is the state's biggest equity challenge, and so far no one has identified a way to apply the power of the Vermont Constitution's common benefits clause to force a judicial solution. Perhaps, though, we shouldn't be waiting for a court to tell us what we already know we should be doing. The language of the common benefits clause is clear. The aspirations and beliefs of Vermont's founders should provide fuel enough to power an engine for change.

Epilogue

I remember watching the online stream in June 2015 of Vermont Senator Bernard Sanders' announcement that he was running to be the Democratic Party nominee for president. The event took place on the Burlington waterfront on a beautiful late-spring day.

Despite the spectacular setting and a feeling of jubilation, Sanders' bid seemed a fool's errand to me. Hillary Clinton's campaign was greased, gassed up, and ready to go. Sanders' chances of winning the nomination were judged to be only a few points above zero. What could he possibly offer that would turn people's attention away from her, a national and international personality, and onto him, a Vermont personality with limited national exposure?

The answer was what Vermonters had been hearing from Sanders for thirty years — the rock-steady message that inequality is growing in America and that something should be done about it. America's middle class is shrinking, causing poverty rates to soar and more children to be deemed food-insecure. Large numbers of Americans lack adequate health care, fewer and fewer workers have pensions, and the homeless can be seen on the streets of virtually every city and town. It was vintage Sanders. We are moving from a society where every person counts to one where the rich and powerful have captured the political parties and turned government into a tool benefiting the One Percent. Differences based on race, ethnicity, gender, and religion are used to divide the country.

Researching this book has convinced me that while Sanders' message may seem deeply personal and its expression uniquely "Bernie," it didn't germinate solely from his individual circumstances and personal reflection. His message, which has gone on to resonate nationally, during two presidential campaigns, has been nurtured in Vermont's political soil, a soil rich in concern for justice and equality. That Sanders would emerge as a voice for equity is not chance or serendipity. Whatever political ideologies Bernie Sanders may espouse, he's also reflecting the vision of the state he moved to as a young man.

Equal is equal, fair is fair. Vermont has been shaped by a history that includes a strong belief that a society's benefits be shared equitably among citizens. Three times in the last twenty years, Vermont has asked that this vision be made real in three very difficult areas of the modern society in which we live — paying for the education of children, understanding and respecting the sexual orientation of others, and taking care of those in need of medical services. We've succeeded in two of these ventures but are still struggling to succeed in the third. The inability to revamp health care is disappointing.

I recall the difficulties after the *Brigham* decision was handed down and Act 60 was met with stiff resistance in some communities. I remember the big white signs with the black letters "Take Back Vermont" after the civil unions bill was passed.

The reality is that there is often a wide gulf between believing in equity and acting to make the belief real. A belief is an aspiration and does not, of and by itself, force change. A law enacted or a court opinion delivered to make the belief real *does* force change, and it can cut deep.

Perhaps the scale of change needed to create an equitable health care system has made too many people too uncomfortable. We are reluctant to leap to a new way of delivering health care despite general agreement we pay too much for health care that sometimes isn't as good as what people in other countries receive at a lower cost.

A court may not be demanding that we take the leap, but our state constitution's common benefits clause strongly encourages us to do so. Not to do so is to accept the lack of equitable access to a benefit whose existence can literally spell life or death for someone. It's a circumstance we should all find intolerable.

Such a circumstance became all too real in 2020 when the COVID-19 virus caused a pandemic that killed more than 500,000 and brought the world's economies to a near standstill. The U.S. was particularly hard hit, surpassing 100,000 deaths before summer began. Numerous hospitals were overwhelmed. Most businesses closed, many workers were laid off, schools shut down, and people were told to stay home. A feeling of vulnerability descended on the country.

Few times so clearly illustrated the need for a robust health care system that serves everyone. T-shirts sold online said the obvious: "We're all in this together."

Could the pandemic be the spur that advances health care reform in Vermont? Might it have provided the moment when it becomes obvious that only a health care system that includes everyone and that everyone can afford is essential to residents' well-being and to the state's prosperity?

It may be useful to think of the approach Amestoy utilized in his opinion in the *Baker* case as a guide to the sort of public discussion and engagement needed to move forward on meaningful health care reform.

"Courts do best by proceeding in a way that is catalytic rather than preclusive," he said.

Perhaps, then, public discussion of health care issues should aim not at what we can't do, but what we want to do and feel that we should do as our responsibility to ourselves, family, friends, and strangers — all citizens of our state, in other words. The basis for doing this is the same as Amestoy saw for the court's involvement — as "courts are participants in the system of democratic deliberation," so certainly are citizens.

And with an approach defined, Amestoy noted the goal: "a paramount objective of a judicial opinion must be persuasiveness." And by "persuasiveness," Amestoy said one must strive toward a resonance with those affected: the message "must in its use of history, text, analysis, and language resonate with those who — to return to my architectural analogy — live in the house and have the power to alter it." Amestoy summarized the process by reflecting on the court action that led to equal marriage rights:

> *[T]he* Baker *opinion was intended to resonate with every Vermonter. For in our constitutional system, every Vermonter is a participant and we all live in the same house. We will know we have built well when — in the words of the poet —* "underneath that roof there was no distinction of persons, but one family only, one heart, one hearth, and one household."[64]

Peter Welch, who pushed for education funding reform over many years in the Vermont legislature before winning election to Congress, said in 1997 of the *Brigham* case, "At a time in our political life in this country when individual success and Darwinian individual survival are celebrated, the *Brigham* case reinforces the fundamental human condition that we are all in this together."[65]

That's what a commitment to equity, as enshrined in our state's constitution, does. It forces us to confront and, we may hope, to act on the discomfort that while we may all be in this together, some have still been left out. When we act to include everyone, we show that in our society, everyone does indeed count.

If Vermont succeeds in building a health care system that meets the needs of all at a cost we can afford, we will reaffirm the state's core belief that equal is equal, and fair is fair. Our forebears would, I feel sure, applaud. And we can honor individuals such as Vermont Supreme Court Justice Thomas Hayes and citizen health care advocate Doctor Deb Richter, *Brigham* attorney Robert Gensburg, *Baker* plaintiffs Stan Baker, Peter Harrigan, Holly Puterbaugh, Lois Farnham, Nina Beck, and Stacy Jolles, and legislators Sally Conrad, Karen Kitzmiller, and Cheryl Rivers who all said, through their work, "We can — and must — do this."

Notes

[1] Finkel, Ken. "How High Was Up? A History of Philadelphia's 'Gentlemen's Agreement.'" *The Philly History Blog, Discoveries from the City Archives,* the City of Philadelphia, June 25, 2013. https://www.phillyhistory.org/blog/index.php/2013/06/how-high-was-up-a-history-of-philadelphias-gentlemans-agreement/

[2] Graffagnino, J. Kevin, Samuel B. Hand, and Gene Sessions, eds. *Vermont Voices, 1609 Through the 1990s: A Documentary History of the Green Mountain State.* Montpelier, Vt.: Vermont Historical Society, 1999.

[3] *State v. Jewett.* Case no. 83-478; 500 A.2d 233 (1985). http://law.justia.com/cases/vermont/supreme-court/1985/83-478-0.html

[4] Chaput, Erik J. "'The Rhode Island Question': The Career of a Debate," *Rhode Island History*, vol. 68, vo. 2, Summer/Fall 2010; online at http://www.rihs.org/assetts/files/publications/2010_SumFall.pdf There was no full biography of Dorr nor full account of the "Dorr Rebellion" itself until 2014, when Chaput expanded on his 2010 article and published *The People's Martyr.* In both the article and his book, Chaput skillfully places the rebellion in the context of national events of the time..

[5] Curti, Merle E. *The Social Ideas of American Educators.* Paterson, N.J.: Pageant Books, 1959. Curti's book began as a report written by the Smith College history professor for the American Historical Association

Commission on the Social Studies in the Schools. The book includes a section on Henry Barnard's life and his accomplishments in promoting public education, not just in Rhode Island but around the country. The book was originally published in 1935; subsequent editions followed, the last in 1965. The text of the 1959 edition can be found online at https://archive.org/stream/socialideaofamer011225mbp/socialideaofamer011225mbp The section on Barnard begins on p. 138; a recounting of his years as Rhode Island education commissioner begins on p. 165. This was the only extensive biographical sketch available of Barnard and his work when I wrote my college senior thesis in 1973. Two biographies followed shortly thereafter: Downs, Robert B., *Henry Barnard* (Boston: Twayne, 1977); and MacMullen, Edith N., *In the Cause of True Education: Henry Barnard and Nineteenth-Century School Reform* (New Haven: Yale University Press, 1991), with MacMullen's book considered the "first full-scale biography of Barnard" (Library Journal).

[6] *BLS History.* https://www.bls.org/m/pages/?uREC_ID=206116&type=d

[7] *The University of Vermont: History and Traditions.* https://www.uvm.edu/history_and_traditions

[8] *Williams v. School District No. 6,* 33 Vt. 271, 274-75 (1860).

[9] Doyle, William. *The Vermont Political Tradition: And Those Who Helped Make It.* Montpelier, Vt.: William Doyle, 1984.

[10] Governors' inaugural and farewell addresses can be accessed at the Vermont Archives and Records Administration collection at 1078 Route 2, Middlesex, Vt. The addresses used to be online at the Office of the Secretary of State's website, but that was no longer the case as of May 2020.

[11] Sautter, John A. "Equity and History: Vermont's Education Revolution of the Early 1890s." *Vermont History,* vol. 76, no. 1, Winter/Spring 2008. https://vermonthistory.org/journal/76/VHS760101_1-18.pdf

[12] "U.S. Immigrant Population and Share over Time, 1850-Present," Migration Policy Institute. https://www.migrationpolicy.org/programs/data-hub/charts/immigrant-population-over-time
Vermont's population at the time of the 1890 census was only 332,422. "Resident Population and Apportionment of the U.S. House of Representatives," U.S. Census Bureau. https://www.census.gov/dmd/www/resapport/states/vermont.pdf
It's unclear what "rate" Page was referring to in his address.

[13] "A Very Short History of Education Finance Prior to the Brigham Decision," Vermont Legislature Joint Fiscal Office. https://legislature.vermont.gov/Documents/2018/WorkGroups/House%20Education/Education%20Finance/W~Mark%20Perrault~A%20Very%20Short%20History%20of%20Education%20Finance%20Prior%20to%20the%20Brigham%20Decision~2-8-2017.pdf

[14] Nelson, John A. "Adequacy in Education: An Analysis of the Constitutional Standard in Vermont," *Vermont Law Review*, vol. 18, no. 1, Fall 1993.

[15] *1997 ACLU of Vermont Annual Report*. Montpelier, Vt.: American Civil Liberties Union Foundation of Vermont, 1998.

[16] Davis, Hamilton E. *Mocking Justice: America's Biggest Drug Scandal*. New York: Crown Publishers, 1968. Davis shows how Lawrence, a crooked cop, was able to move around Vermont, from one police department to another, and evade investigation for years. Gensburg enters the book on p. 173.

[17] Robert Gensburg obituary. *Caledonian Record*, St. Johnsbury, Vt., Nov. 14, 2017. https://www.caledonianrecord.com/community/deaths/robert-gensburg---obituary/article_50693cce-c957-5a02-89cd-b3a9727594af.html
Also, Gensburg & Greaves, PLLC, law firm, professional resume for Robert A. Gensburg. https://www.gensburgandgreaves.com/attorney-profiles/robert-gensburg/

[18] O'Gradey, Patrick. "N.H. School Funding Is Up For Discussion." *Valley News*, Aug. 5, 2018. https://www.vnews.com/Atrorneys-come-to-Newport-to-talk-about-state-s-obligation-on-education-funding-19249884

[19] *Brigham v. State*. Case no. 96-502; 166 Vt. 246, 692 A.2d 384 (1997). The full text of the *Brigham v. State* decision can be found at https://law.justia.com/cases/vermont/supreme-court/1997/96-502op.html

[20] The full text of Act 60 can be found online at the Vermont legislative website: http://www.leg.state.vt.us/DOCS/1998/ACTS/ACT060.HTM

[21] Goldberg, Carey. "School Tax Law Splits 'Haves' and 'Have Nots.'" *The New York Times*, Dec. 19, 1997: A34.

[22] Burkett, Elinor. "Don't Tread on My Tax Rate." *The New York Times Magazine*, April 26, 1998: 42–45. The article can be found online at https://www.nytimes.com/1998/04/26/magazine/dont-tread-on-my-tax-rate.html

[23] Gensburg, Robert. "Testimony of Atty Bob Gensburg to Ways and Means Committee, January 11, 2001."

[24] "School finance equity" is a fraught equation, leading to sophisticated statistical analysis and complicated financial calculations. In 2011, Vermont commissioned a nationally known expert in the field of school finance, Prof. Larry Picus of the University of Southern California, to analyze the equity of Vermont's K-12 system. His 285-page report is a thorough examination of numerous topics, including school finance equity. On that subject, he concluded: "We find that using standard school finance equity statistics of fiscal neutrality and per pupil expenditure equality Vermont fares very well. Analyses of the wealth elasticity of the system — the relationship between measures of wealth and levels of per pupil spending — show that whether measured by property wealth or income, there is little relationship between wealth and the level of per pupil spending across Vermont school districts.

We also found that education spending per pupil has increased significantly over the past decade, but that statistical measures of spending disparities have actually improved. This finding suggests that the states' choice to not limit the level of spending any town can choose has not led either to wide disparities in spending or to inordinate increases in spending either by previously low spending or low fiscal capacity districts." Lawrence O. Picus And Associates. An Analysis of Vermont's Education Finance System, submitted to Vermont Joint Fiscal Office, Jan. 18, 2012. http://picusodden. com/wp-content/uploads/2013/09/VT_Finance_Study_1-18-2012.pdf

[25] Budbill, David. "William Parker, David Budbill And Act 60." *Sunday Rutland Herald and Times Argus*, Nov. 1, 1998, Commentary section.

[26] Sean Reardon, professor of poverty and inequality in education at the Stanford Graduate School of Education, points out that the gap between low- and high-income American families has grown substantially in the past fifty years. With it has come a greater gap in student achievement between the rich and poor. Schools "cannot be expected to solve this problem on their own, but they must be part of the solution," he wrote in a 2011 essay, "The Widening Academic Achievement Gap Between the Rich and the Poor: New Evidence and Possible Explanations." Stanford University, July 2011. https://cepa.stanford.edu/sites/default/files/reardon%20whither%20 opportunity%20-%20chapter%205.pdf

[27] Pache, Tiffany Danitz. "Report sees growing inequality playing out in schools." *VTDigger.org*, May 16, 2016. http://vtdigger.org/2016/05/16/report- sees-growing-inequality-playing-out-in-schools/

[28] Russakoff, Dale. *The Prize: Who's in Charge of America's Schools?* Boston and New York: Houghton Mifflin Harcourt, 2015.

[29] Russakoff, p. 119.

[30] Dorfman, Dorinne. "Testimony to the Vermont House Education Committee Regarding Act 46." Nov. 18, 2015.

[31] "Theodore Parker And The 'Moral Universe.'" *All Things Considered,* NPR, Sept. 2, 2013. https://www.npr.org/templates/story/story.php?storyId=129609461

[32] For much of the information here and in following paragraphs, I've relied on two books: Mello, Michael. *Legalizing Gay Marriage: Vermont and the National Debate.* Philadelphia: Temple University Press, 2008; and Moats, David. *Civil Wars, A Battle For Gay Marriage.* Orlando, Fl.: Harcourt, 2004.

[33] *Baker v. State.* Case no. 98-032; 170 Vt. 194, 744 A.2d 864, 81 A.L.R.5th 627 (1999). The full text of the *Baker v. State* decision can be found at https://www.lambdalegal.org/in-court/legal-docs/baker_vt_19991220_decision-vt-supreme-court

[34] A detailed account of the legislature's deliberations and votes on the bill can be found in Ch. 7, "Act Anew," of Moats's book, *Civil Wars.*

[35] Cyrus, Connor. "Couple at forefront of Vt. civil union fight reflect on journey." Burlington, Vt., WCAX TV, June 28, 2019. A print version can be found at https://www.wcax.com/content/news/Vermont-couple-who-sued-for-legal-recognition-reflects-on-fight-for-marriage-equality-511944831.html

[36] Rosin, Hanna. "Same-Sex Union Divides Small Vermont Community." *Washington Post*, Oct. 11, 2000. https://www.washingtonpost.com/archive/politics/2000/10/11/same-sex-union-divides-small-vermont-community/8b4e1820-6798-4601-9211-847a1c94b940/

[37] Robinson, Kate. "As a moderate Republican, Mallary prized compromise and bipartisanship." *VTDigger.org*, Oct. 3, 2011. https://vtdigger.org/2011/10/03/mallary/

[38] *Poe v. Ullman*, 367 US 497 (1961). https://www.oyez.org/cases/1960/60

[39] Amestoy, Jeffrey L. "Pragmatic Constitutionalism — Reflections on State Constitutional Theory and Same-Sex Marriage Claims." *Rutgers Law Journal*, vol. 35, no. 4, 2004, 1249.

[40] Reed, Douglas S. "Popular Constitutionalism: Toward a Theory of State Constitutional Meanings." *Rutgers Law Journal*, vol. 30, no. 4, 1999.

[41] G. Alan Tarr, a political science professor at Rutgers, served as director of the Center for State Constitutional Studies when his book *Understanding State Constitutions* was published by Princeton University Press in 1998.

[42] Amestoy, 1257.

[43] *Baker* (quoting Sunstein, Cass R. "Foreword: Leaving Things Undecided," *Harvard Law Review*, vol. 110, no. 4, 1996, 101).

[44] Amestoy, 1261–62.

[45] *Amestoy* (quoting Longfellow, Henry Wadsworth. "Tales of a Wayside Inn, The Theologian's Tale: Elizabeth," in *Longfellow's Complete Poems*. Boston: Houghton, Mifflin & Co., 1902.)

[46] Wright, Ralph. *All Politics is Personal.* Manchester, Vt.: Marshall Jones Company, 1996, 223.

[47] Wright, 225.

[48] Lallemand, Nicole Cafarella, and Judy Feder. "Health Care Stewardship: Vermont Case Study." Urban Institute Health Policy Center, January 2016. http://www.urban.org/sites/default/files/publication/76931/2000583-Health-Care-Stewardship-Vermont-Case-Study.pdf

49 Fandos, Nicholas. "HSPH Professor Helps with Vermont Health Care Reform." *The Harvard Crimson,* Dec. 7, 2011. https://www.thecrimson.com/article/2011/12/7/hsia-health-care-vermont/

50 Sanford, Gregory. "Aunt Serena Tackles Health Care Costs," June 2005. This was an article in a series by Sanford, former Vermont state archivist, called *Voice from the Vault.* The series can be viewed at the Vermont Archives and Records Administration at 1078 Route 2, Middlesex, Vt. Some of the articles are also online at the Office of the Secretary of State's website. The "Aunt Serena" article can be found at https://sos.vermont.gov/media/kfihrebj/auntserenatackleshealthcarecosts.pdf

51 Sanford, "Socialized Medicine: The View from 1944" in *Voice from the Vault,* 2009. https://sos.vermont.gov/media/kvid5fg3/opinions_voicefromthevault_may2009.pdf

52 Roosevelt, Franklin D. "Second Bill of Rights" speech. https://www.youtube.com/watch?v=3EZ5bx9AyI4

53 Truman, Harry S. "Letter on Health Care," April 12, 1949. National Archives, Harry S. Truman Presidential Library and Museum. http://recordsofrights.org/records/129/letter-from-harry-s-truman-on-health-care

54 A good source of information about health care reform efforts in Vermont in the 1970s, '80s, and early '90s is the article "Vermont: Health Care Reform in Vermont: A Work in Progress" by Howard M. Leichter. It appeared in the journal *Health Affairs*, vol. 12, no. 2, January 1993. Available on the web at https://www.healthaffairs.org/doi/10.1377/hlthaff.12.2.71

55 "Report of the Vermont Blue-Ribbon Commission on Health," January 1992, cited in Leichter.

56 "The Jail Health-Care Crisis" by Steve Coll, *The New Yorker,* March 4, 2019, 31.

[57] Papanicolas, Irene, Liana R. Woskie, and Ashish Jha. "Health Care Spending in the United States and Other High-Income Countries." Commonwealth Fund, March 13, 2018. Online at https://www.commonwealthfund.org/publications/journal-article/2018/mar/health-care-spending-united-states-and-other-high-income This report was followed up two years later by a Commonwealth Fund issue brief on a similar topic: Tikkanen, Roosa and Melinda K. Abrams. "U.S. Health Care from a Global Perspective, 2019: Higher Spending, Worse Outcomes?" https://www.commonwealthfund.org/publications/issue-briefs/2020/jan/us-health-care-global-perspective-2019

[58] Ollove was writing for the Pew Charitable Trust's "Stateline" news reporting initiative, which focuses on state-level actions on fiscal, health, demographic, and government issues. A *PBS NewsHour* segment based on Ollove's report, "How This Vermont Experiment Improves Patient Health at Lower Cost," aired March 2, 2017. http://www.pbs.org/newshour/rundown/vermont-experiment-improves-patient-health-lower-cost/

[59] Fisher, Michael, Kaili Kuiper, Eric Schultheis, and Julia Shaw. "Letter from Office of the Health Care Advocate to Green Mountain Care Board," Nov. 9, 2018. https://gmcboard.vermont.gov/sites/gmcb/files/HCA%20Comments%20OneCare%20VT%202019%20Budget%20Review%2011-9-18.pdf

[60] "Joint Resolution Relating to the Creation of a Commission on Public Health Care Values and Priorities." No. R-181, 1993–1994 Vermont legislative session. http://www.leg.state.vt.us/DOCS/1994/ACTS/ACTR181.HTM

[61] *Understanding Health Care: An Introduction to Vermont's Health Care System*. Commission on the Public's Health Care Values and Priorities. Vermont, 2001.

[62] President Calvin Coolidge, "Address Before the American Legion Convention at Omaha, Nebraska," Oct. 6, 1925. American Presidency Project. https://www.presidency.ucsb.edu/documents/address-before-the-american-legion-convention-omaha-nebraska

[63] Kolbert, Elizabeth. "Why Facts Don't Change Our Minds." *The New Yorker,* Feb. 20, 2017. https://www.newyorker.com/magazine/2017/02/27/why-facts-dont-change-our-minds

[64] Amestoy, "Pragmatic Constitutionalism," 1261–62.

[65] Welch, Peter. Comments in "Revolutionizing Education In Vermont: How it All Came About," *1997 ACLU of Vermont Annual Report.*

Sources

"Act 60, Equal Educational Opportunity Act of 1997." 1997-1998 Vermont legislative session. *leg.state.vt.us,* http://www.leg.state.vt.us/ DOCS/1998/ACTS/ACT060.HTM Accessed April 29, 2020.

"Acts Of The 1993-1994 Vermont Legislature." *leg.state.vt.us,* http://www.leg. state.vt.us/DOCS/1994/ACTS/ACTR181.HTM Accessed April 27, 2020.

Amestoy, Jeffrey L. "Pragmatic Constitutionalism — Reflections on State Constitutional Theory and Same-Sex Marriage Claims." *Rutgers Law Journal,* vol. 35, no. 4, 2004.

Baker v. State of Vermont. Case no. 98-032; 170 Vt. 194, 744 A.2d 864, 81 A.L.R.5th 627 (1999). *lambdalegal.org,* https://www.lambdalegal.org/ in-court/legal-docs/baker_vt_19991220_decision-vt-supreme-court Accessed April 27, 2020.

BLS-History: Boston Latin School-Boston Latin School Association. bls.org, https://www.bls.org/m/pages/?uREC_ID=206116&type=d Accessed April 27, 2020.

Brigham v. State of Vermont. Case no. 96-502; 166 Vt. 246, 692 A.2d 384 (1997). *justia.com,* https://law.justia.com/cases/vermont/supreme-court/1997/96-502op.html Accessed April 27, 2020.

Budbill, David. "William Parker, David Budbill And Act 60." *Sunday Rutland Herald and Times Argus*, Nov. 1, 1998, Commentary section.

Burkett, Elinor. "Don't Tread on My Tax Rate." *The New York Times Magazine*, April 26, 1998. *nytimes.com*, https://www.nytimes.com/1998/04/26/magazine/dont-tread-on-my-tax-rate.html Accessed April 27, 2020.

Chaput, Erik J. "'The Rhode Island Question': The Career of a Debate." *Rhode Island History*, vol. 68, no. 2, Summer/Fall 2010. *rihs.org*, http://www.rihs.org/assetts/files/publications/2010_SumFall.pdf Accessed April 27, 2020.

Coll, Steve. "The Jail Health-Care Crisis." *The New Yorker*, March 4, 2019. *newyorker.com*, https://www.newyorker.com/magazine/2019/03/04/the-jail-health-care-crisis Accessed April 27, 2020.

Coolidge, Calvin. "Address Before the American Legion Convention at Omaha, Nebraska." American Presidency Project. *presidency.ucsb.edu,* https://www.presidency.ucsb.edu/documents/address-before-the-american-legion-convention-omaha-nebraska Accessed April 27, 2020.

Curti, Merle E. *The Social Ideas Of American Educators*. Paterson, N.J.: Pageant Books, 1959. *archive.org*, http://archive.org/details/socialideaofamer011225mbp Accessed April 27, 2020.

Cyrus, Connor. "Couple at Forefront of Vt. Civil Union Fight Reflect on Journey." Burlington, Vt., WCAX TV, June 28, 2019. *wcax.com,* https://www.wcax.com/content/news/Vermont-couple-who-sued-for-legal-recognition-reflects-on-fight-for-marriage-equality-511944831.html Accessed April 27, 2020.

Davis, Hamilton E. *Mocking Justice: Vermont's Biggest Drug Scandal.* New York: Crown Publishers, 1968.

Dorfman, Dorinne. "Testimony to the Vermont House Education Committee Regarding Act 46," Nov. 18, 2015, author's copy of printed testimony distributed at hearing.

Doyle, William. *The Vermont Political Tradition: And Those Who Helped Make It.* Montpelier, Vt.: William Doyle, 1984.

An Evaluation of Vermont's Education Finance System. picusodden.com, http://picusodden.com/wp-content/uploads/2013/09/VT_Finance_ Study_1-18-2012.pdf Accessed April 27, 2020.

Fandos, Nicholas. "HSPH Professor Helps with Vermont Health Care Reform." *The Harvard Crimson*, Dec. 7, 2011. *thecrimson.com*, https:// www.thecrimson.com/article/2011/12/7/hsia-health-care-vermont/ Accessed April 27, 2020.

Finkel, Ken. "How High Was Up? A History of Philadelphia's 'Gentleman's Agreement.'" *The Philly History Blog, Discoveries from the City Archives*, the City of Philadelphia, June 25, 2013. *www.phillyhistory. org*, https://www.phillyhistory.org/blog/index.php/2013/06/how-high-was-up-a-history-of-philadelphias-gentlemans-agreement/ Accessed April 27, 2020.

Fisher, Michael, Kaili Kuiper, Eric Schultheis, and Julia Shaw. "Letter from Office of the Health Care Advocate to Green Mountain Care Board," Nov. 9, 2018. *gmcboard.vermont.gov*, https://gmcboard.vermont. gov/sites/gmcb/files/HCA%20Comments%20OneCare%20VT%20 2019%20Budget%20Review%2011-9-18.pdf Accessed April 27, 2020.

Gensburg, Robert. "Testimony of Atty Bob Gensburg to Ways and Means Committee," Jan. 11, 2001, author's copy of printed testimony distributed at hearing.

Goldberg, Carey. "School Tax Law Splits 'Haves' and 'Have Nots.'" *The New York Times*, Dec. 19, 1997. *nytimes.com*, https://www.nytimes.com/1997/12/19/us/school-tax-law-splits-haves-and-have-nots.html Accessed April 27, 2020.

Graffagnino, J. Kevin, Samuel B. Hand, and Gene Sessions, eds. *Vermont Voices, 1609 Through the 1990s: A Documentary History of the Green Mountain State*. Montpelier, Vt.: Vermont Historical Society, 1999.

"Joint Resolution Relating to the Creation of a Commission on Public Health Care Values and Priorities." No. R-181, 1993-1994 Vermont legislative session. *leg.state.vt.us*, http://www.leg.state.vt.us/DOCS/1994/ACTS/ACTR181.HTM Accessed March 30, 2020.

Kolbert, Elizabeth. "Why Facts Don't Change Our Minds." *The New Yorker*, Feb. 20, 2017. *newyorker.com*, https://www.newyorker.com/magazine/2017/02/27/why-facts-dont-change-our-minds Accessed April 27, 2020.

Lallemand, Nicole Cafarella, and Judy Feder. "Health Care Stewardship: Vermont Case Study." Urban Institute Health Policy Center, January 2016. *urban.org*, http://www.urban.org/sites/default/files/publication/76931/2000583-Health-Care-Stewardship-Vermont-Case-Study.pdf Accessed April 27, 2020.

Leichter, Howard M. "Vermont: Health Care Reform in Vermont: A Work in Progress." *Health Affairs*, vol. 12, no. 2, January 1993, Project HOPE: The People-to-People Health Foundation, Inc. *healthaffairs.org*, https://www.healthaffairs.org/doi/10.1377/hlthaff.12.2.71 Accessed April 27, 2020.

Mello, Michael. *Legalizing Gay Marriage: Vermont And The National Debate.* Philadelphia, Pa.: Temple University Press, 2008.

Moats, David. *Civil Wars: A Battle for Gay Marriage.* Orlando, Fl.: Harcourt, 2004.

Nelson, John A. "Adequacy in Education: An Analysis of the Constitutional Standard in Vermont," *Vermont Law Review*, vol. 18, no. 1, Fall 1993.

O'Gradey, Patrick. "N.H. School Funding Is Up For Discussion." *Valley News*, Aug. 5, 2018. *vnews.com*, https://www.vnews.com/Atrorneys-come-to-Newport-to-talk-about-state-s-obligation-on-education-funding-19249884 Accessed April 27, 2020.

Ollove, Michael. "How This Vermont Experiment Improves Patient Health at Lower Cost." *PBS NewsHour*, March 2, 2017. *pbs.org*, https://www.pbs.org/newshour/health/vermont-experiment-improves-patient-health-lower-cost Accessed April 27, 2020.

Pache, Tiffany Danitz. "Report sees growing inequality playing out in schools." *VTDigger*, May 16, 2016. *vtdigger.org*, https://vtdigger.org/2016/05/16/report-sees-growing-inequality-playing-out-in-schools/ Accessed April 27, 2020.

Papanicolas, Irene, Liana R. Woskie, and Ashish Jha. *Health Care Spending in US, Other High-Income Countries.* Commonwealth Fund, March 13, 2018. *commonwealthfund.org*, https://www.commonwealthfund.org/publications/journal-article/2018/mar/health-care-spending-united-states-and-other-high-income Accessed April 27, 2020.

Picus, Lawrence O., and Associates. "An Analysis of Vermont's Education
     Finance System," submitted to Vermont Joint Fiscal Office, Jan.
     18, 2012. *picusodden.com*, http://picusodden.com/wp-content/
     uploads/2013/09/VT_Finance_Study_1-18-2012.pdf Accessed March
     17, 2020.

Poe v. Ullman. 367 U.S. 497 (1961). *oyez.org,* https://www.oyez.org/
     cases/1960/60 Accessed April 30, 2020.

Reardon, Sean. "The Widening Academic Achievement Gap Between
     the Rich and the Poor: New Evidence and Possible Explanations."
     Stanford University, July 2011. *stanford.edu*, https://cepa.stanford.
     edu/sites/default/files/reardon%20whither%20opportunity%20
     -%20chapter%205.pdf Accessed April 28, 2020.

Reed, Douglas S. "Popular Constitutionalism: Towards a Theory of State
     Constitutional Meanings." *Rutgers Law Journal*, vol. 30, no. 4, 1999.

Report of the Vermont Blue-Ribbon Commission on Health. Vermont, 1992.

"Resident Population and Apportionment of the U.S. House of
     Representatives," U.S. Census Bureau. *census.gov*, https://www.
     census.gov/dmd/www/resapport/states/vermont.pdf Accessed May
     11, 2020.

"Robert A. Gensburg Obituary." *Caledonian Record*, St. Johnsbury, Vt., Nov.
     14, 2017. *caledonianrecord.com,* https://www.caledonianrecord.com/
     community/deaths/robert-gensburg---obituary/article_50693cce-
     c957-5a02-89cd-b3a9727594af.html Also, Gensburg & Greaves, PLLC,
     law firm, *attorney profile* for Robert A. Gensburg. *gensburgandgreaves.
     com*, https://www.gensburgandgreaves.com/attorney-profiles/robert-
     gensburg/ Both accessed March 25, 2020.

Robinson, Kate. "As a moderate Republican, Mallary prized compromise and bipartisanship." *VTDigger*, Oct. 3, 2011. *vtdigger.org*, https://vtdigger. org/2011/10/03/mallary/ Accessed April 27, 2020.

Roosevelt, Franklin D. "Second Bill of Rights," *youtube.com*, https://www. youtube.com/watch?v=3EZ5bx9AyI4 Accessed April 27, 2020.

Rosin, Hanna. "Same-Sex Union Divides Small Vermont Community." *Washington Post*, Oct. 11, 2000. *washingtonpost.com*, https://www. washingtonpost.com/archive/politics/2000/10/11/same-sex-union-divides-small-vermont-community/8b4e1820-6798-4601-9211-847a1c94b940/ Accessed April 27, 2020.

Russakoff, Dale. *The Prize: Who's in Charge of America's Schools?* Boston and New York: Houghton Mifflin, Harcourt, 2015.

Sanford, Gregory. "Socialized Medicine: The View from 1944" in *Voice from the Vault* series, May 2009. *sos.vermont.gov*, https://sos.vermont.gov/ media/kvid5fg3/opinions_voicefromthevault_may2009.pdf Accessed April 27, 2020.

Sanford, Gregory. "Aunt Serena Tackles Health Care Cost" in *Voice from the Vault* series, June 2005. *sos.vermont.gov*, https://sos.vermont.gov/ media/kfihrebj/auntserenatackleshealthcarecosts.pdf Accessed April 27, 2020.

Sautter, John A. "Equity and History: Vermont's Education Revolution in the Early 1890s." *Vermont History*, vol. 76, no. 1, Winter/Spring 2008. *vermonthistory.org*, https://vermonthistory.org/journal/76/ VHS760101_1-18.pdf Accessed April 27, 2020.

State v. Jewett. Case no. 83-478; 500 A.2d 233 (1985). *law.justia.com,* http:// law.justia.com/cases/vermont/supreme-court/1985/83-478-0.html Accessed April 28, 2020.

Sunstein, Cass R. "Foreword: Leaving Things Undecided," *Harvard Law Review*, vol. 110, no. 4, 1996, 101.

Tarr, G. Alan. *Understanding State Constitutions*. Princeton, N.J.: Princeton University Press, 2000.

"Theodore Parker And The 'Moral Universe.'" *All Things Considered*, NPR, Sept. 2, 2010. *npr.org*, https://www.npr.org/templates/story/story.php?storyId=129609461 Accessed March 29, 2020.

Tikkanen, Roosa, and Melinda K. Abrams. "U.S. Health Care from a Global Perspective, 2019: Higher Spending, Worse Outcomes?" Commonwealth Fund, Jan. 30, 2020. *commonwealthfund.org*, https://www.commonwealthfund.org/publications/issue-briefs/2020/jan/us-health-care-global-perspective-2019 Accessed April 27, 2020.

Truman, Harry S. "Letter on Health Care," April 12, 1949. National Archives, Harry S. Truman Presidential Library and Museum. *recordsofrights.org*, http://recordsofrights.org/records/129/letter-from-harry-s-truman-on-health-care Accessed April 27, 2020.

Understanding Health Care: An Introduction to Vermont's Health Care System. Commission on the Public's Health Care Values and Priorities. Vermont, 2001.

The University of Vermont: History and Traditions. uvm.edu, https://www.uvm.edu/history_and_traditions Accessed April 28, 2020.

"U.S. Immigrant Population and Share over Time, 1850-Present, Migration Policy Institute. *migrationpolicy.org*, https://www.migrationpolicy.org/programs/data-hub/charts/immigrant-population-over-time Accessed May 11, 2020.

"A Very Short History of Education Finance Prior to the Brigham Decision."
Vermont Legislature Joint Fiscal Office. *legislature.vermont.gov*,
https://legislature.vermont.gov/Documents/2018/WorkGroups/
House%20Education/Education%20Finance/W~Mark%20
Perrault~A%20Very%20Short%20History%20of%20Education%20
Finance%20Prior%20to%20the%20Brigham%20Decision~2-8-2017.
pdf Accessed April 27, 2020.

Welch, Peter. Comments in "Revolutionizing Education in Vermont: How it
All Came About," *1997 ACLU of Vermont Annual Report*. Montpelier,
Vt.: American Civil Liberties Union Foundation of Vermont, 1998.

Williams v. School District No. 6, 33 Vt. 271, 274-75 (1860).

Wright, Ralph. *All Politics Is Personal*. Manchester Center, Vt.: Marshall
Jones Co., 1996.

Acknowledgements

A number of years ago, when I was working as assistant editor at the *Sunday Rutland Herald-Times Argus,* a colleague, Jeff Danziger, was setting up a publishing business. He had ideas for lots of books. "Do you have a book in you?" he asked me late one Friday night as we were sharing drinks after a long evening of editing (me) and cartooning (him). I said I hoped to write a book at some point in my life, but for now I was pretty pre-occupied with editing, and writing an occasional feature story or column.

I did write a book for German students learning English; after seven years at the *Herald-Argus,* I landed a job teaching English studies at a German university, and a school-book publisher was looking for an interesting story about life in America. The assignment came with a very limiting requirement, however: I could only use vocabulary from a list of English words that German students at a certain level of their foreign language studies could be expected to know.

It was a real challenge. I had to sketch out characters, setting, and a plot of sorts. And then I had to start writing, all the while checking the list of acceptable words to make sure the readability level was appropriate.

It was hard to think of this as a book that "I had in me." But just reaching that conclusion made me feel grateful to Jeff Danziger for introducing me to the notion that our experiences in life bear thoughts, feelings, ideas, and beliefs that crave to be ordered, categorized, and understood – through thinking and writing.

Equal Is Equal, Fair Is Fair is a book that developed in me over many years, as I note in the Introduction. My time as a journalist introduced me to the conundrum, "They can't do that, can they?" It's a conundrum because someone has already done harm to another person. The proper question is, "Can they get away with what they've just done?" I thank journalists Kendall Wild and Glenn Gershaneck for opening the door for me on what accountability means and how it's pursued in questions of equity and fairness.

My time as a teacher showed me many things (not just that sometimes you have to write with a very limited vocabulary). I taught a course at Community College of Vermont one semester titled "American History Through Autobiography." My students were great. They may not have been avid historians, but they loved reading stories of other people's lives. The students were candid about what they knew and what they didn't. One taught me a lesson I've never forgotten. We were talking during one class about the importance of the establishment of the Federal Deposit Insurance Corp. (FDIC). A young woman said she didn't understand why it was necessary. "How can a bank lose the money I put into my savings account?" she asked. "It's put in a drawer with my name on it when I deposit it, and then when I want it back, they just go to that drawer and take it out – and add a little bit of interest." The lesson I learned was this: Never assume that people understand how an institution as simple (or so it seemed to me) as a local bank is, really, quite sophisticated and its practices often incomprehensible to many. Thank you to students who have, through their questions and answers, taught me that one doesn't really understand anything until you can explain it, in adequately simple terms, to others. I hope I've achieved that in this book.

My time at the American Civil Liberties Union was a combination of learning what law school might have been like had I enrolled in one after college, and understanding how the enforcement of laws and the enactment of just policies are not automatic and that people who work in politics and government generally don't lead but follow. For these lessons I have attorney David Putter to thank (he led the ACLU-VT's Legal Advisory Panel for many years) and a number of politicians and government workers I got to know through ACLU work. I am grateful that Vermont politicians generally *do* respond to constituents' concerns. It is how a representative government is supposed to work.

Helping to bring to fruition the book that had been growing within me required the assistance of many people skilled in research, writing, history, and publishing. I am grateful to Rachel Fisher, Paul Gillies, Jack Hoffman, Bernie Lambek, Hope Mathiessen, Gretchen Morse, Chris Noel, Gregory Sanford, Bill Schubart, Michael Sherman, Virginia Lindauer Simmon, and Mason Singer.

Thanks to Amanda Brigham, Kate Baker, Ming Linsley, and Deb Richter, whose stories I tell to give human dimension to the issues described in this book. As plaintiffs or advocates, they have been real agents for change. To me, they are true heroes.

I would like to acknowledge another group of heroes, the Vermont Supreme Court justices who gave unanimous votes to the decisions in both the *Brigham* (school finance) and *Baker* (marriage equality) cases. The only (partial) dissent came, in the *Baker* case, from a justice who agreed the court was making the right ruling but wanted faster action on its application. These five men and two women told us of the constitutional responsibility we have to treat everyone equally and fairly. They are Justices John Dooley, Ernest Gibson III, Denise Johnson, James Morse, and Marilyn Skoglund, and Chief Justices Frederic Allen and Jeffrey Amestoy. May the judges in future "common benefits" cases have equal courage to remind us of our state's commitment to equity.

I was very pleased when David Moats agreed to write the foreword of this book. Former editorial page editor of the *Rutland Herald,* Moats had a ringside seat to many of the events I describe in my book. The Pulitzer Prize he won in 2001 for his editorials on the battle for same-sex marriage rights was richly deserved.

And finally, I wish to acknowledge that although writing a book is a rather solitary process, those around you know you're on a peculiar journey that takes on a life of its own. My wife, Lila Richardson, has quietly assented to my desire to spend hours understanding Act 60, the *Baker* decision, and why Vermont hasn't gotten to where it knows it needs to be regarding health care. Our son, Will, made mind-bogglingly arcane chores like creating endnotes engagingly interesting. Thank you, both.

Allen Gilbert
June 2020

About the Author

ALLEN GILBERT began his professional work as a reporter at the *Rutland Herald* in 1976. He became city editor of the *Herald,* and then assistant editor of the *Sunday Rutland Herald-Times Argus*. He taught writing at several Vermont colleges, and American studies at a German university. For 14 years he was a principal in PressKit of Montpelier, a communications and public policy research firm. He served as executive director of the Vermont affiliate of the American Civil Liberties Union from 2004 to 2016. He was also a regular commentator on Vermont Public Radio.

Gilbert has been active in statewide education issues. He chaired the Worcester School Board when it joined the ACLU's *Brigham* lawsuit, the suit brought to address education funding disparities. He also served on the U-32 High School Board and was president of the Vermont School Boards Association.

Gilbert graduated magna cum laude from Harvard College with a degree in history. He also holds a master's degree in education from the College of William and Mary. He lives in Worcester, Vermont, with his wife, Lila Richardson, a former Vermont Legal Aid attorney. They have two sons, Samuel and William.

CPSIA information can be obtained
at www.ICGtesting.com
Printed in the USA
LVHW030059010622
720159LV00003B/464